Tahoe Place Names

Tahoe
Place Names

The origin and history of names in the Lake Tahoe Basin

Barbara Lekisch

Foreword
Richard H. Dillon

GREAT WEST BOOKS · LAFAYETTE, CALIFORNIA · 1988

Cover design by Larry Van Dyke, Peter Browning, and Barbara Lekisch.
Front cover: Sketch by George H. Goddard in 1855, the first drawing
            made of Lake Tahoe. It was initially printed in *Hutchings'*
            California Magazine, September 1857.
Back cover: Portion of the *Topographical map of Central California,*
            together with a part of Nevada, 1873. State Geological Survey
            of California. Charles F. Hoffmann, Principal Topographer.

Printed in the United States of America

Great West Books
PO Box 1028
Lafayette, CA 94549

Library of Congress Cataloging-in-Publication Data

Lekisch, Barbara, 1942–
    Tahoe place names.

    Bibliography: p.
    1. Names, Geographical—Tahoe, Lake, Region (Calif.
and Nev.) 2. Tahoe, Lake, Region (Calif. and Nev.)—
History, Local. I. Title.
F868.T2L45 1988   979.4'38'00321   88–80574
ISBN 0–944220–01–0 (pbk. : alk. paper)

This book is dedicated to my beloved daughter
Hallie Keppelman
and in memory of
Alberta Vance, Douglas Susens, and Edmund Forder,
with whom we enjoyed so many carefree Tahoe days

Contents

Illustrations

Foreword

Barbara Lekisch's experience as the head librarian at the California Historical Society, and formerly librarian at the Sierra Club, shows in her skillful handling of the nomenclature of the Lake Tahoe Basin. She has created a splendid dictionary—no, an encyclopedia, such is its wonderful detail—of the place names around Lake Tahoe and up to the crest of the surrounding mountains.

Each entry is located not only in its California or Nevada county, but also on its Forest Service or Geological Survey quadrangle map. When possible, each name is also located on important historical maps, such as those of George H. Goddard, the State Geological Survey of California, and the Wheeler Survey. The "definitions" of the place names are enhanced by interesting quotations from early visitors to the scene, often the very namers themselves. These quotes are so well-chosen that *Tahoe Place Names* is not merely a handbook for knapsack or glove compartment (and, of course, a library reference work), but is also a book that is fun to read. The description of Snowshoe Thompson's feats in the Thompson Peak entry, and the discussion of the long-running controversy over whether Lake Tahoe should be named Bonpland, Bigler, or Tahoe are excellent historical and biographical sketches in themselves.

The author, wisely, does not cling tightly to what we might call "tidewater Tahoe." She covers important locations at some distance from the lakeshore if they are geographically or historically related. Some examples are Daggett Pass, Kingsbury Grade, and Genoa; The Dardanelles near Sonora Pass; and Red Lake near Carson Pass.

This book is as much about Tahoe Basin and Sierra Nevada biography as it is about history, geography, and natural history. Lekisch does not skimp on the human landscape of roads and resorts, in addition to streams, peaks, and passes. She describes landmarks from the viewpoint of early Washoe Indians before taking up the observations of explorers, cartographers, squatters, and tourists.

Tahoe has been a sort of Newport-in-the-Ponderosas for San Francisco's elite of wealth and power. The list of summer residents reads like The City's social register: DeYoung, Baldwin, Pope, Holladay, Mills, Sharon, Ralston, Dollar, Lick, Crocker, Hellman, Tevis, Fleischhacker. But even more interesting are such little-known denizens of the fabled "mountain sea" region as Captain Dick Barter, the hermit of Emerald Bay; pioneer resort owner John McKinney; and Mickey Free the bandit.

It is apparent that Lekisch has studied maps, both old and new, as well as whole shelves of documents and books—including old county histories and dusty great registers of voters—not to mention dizzying reels of microfilmed newspapers. The research must have been a prodigious, albeit rewarding, task of historical, bibliographical, and cartographic detective work.

Thanks to this fine effort, we can add the name Lekisch to the roster of place names scholars such as Gudde, Stewart, Farquhar, and Browning. The *story* of Lake Tahoe is here too, in and between the lines. Simply browsing in this volume will make it clear to the reader why Professor Joseph LeConte wrote, many years ago: "I could dream away my life here with those I love. . . . Of all the places I have yet seen, this is the one which I could longest enjoy and love the most."

RICHARD H. DILLON

Preface

My interest in Tahoe place names began when I was hiking with a friend in Desolation Wilderness, and first saw "Jabu," a tiny, exquisite lake near Cracked Crag. "Jabu" remained a mystery until I became the librarian at the Sierra Club in San Francisco. A Sierra Club Library volunteer and long-term member, Harriet T. Parsons, inquired for me through Marjorie Bridge Farquhar and Haven Jorgensen, both of whom have spent many summers at Echo Lake. From them I learned that the name is a composite using the first two letters of a man's first and last names (see **Jabu**).

Francis Bacon wrote: "Name, though it seem but a superficial and outward matter, yet it carrieth much impression and enchantment." Finding Jabu Lake and then the meaning of its name led to many years of enjoyable activity. I began the Tahoe place names project so that my young daughter Hallie and I could sit together evenings doing our homework. The project led me to a six-year-long job at the Sierra Club's William E. Colby Memorial Library. I would go there on my lunch break from the Mechanics' Institute Library in search of names information, and eventually I applied for the job of librarian.

My sincere thanks go to those who encouraged and assisted me in the completion of the project, which began ten years ago. At the top of the list is Peter Browning, editor and publisher, whose extensive assistance makes him a veritable co-author. The many others who helped are Bern Kreissman, who located books and photographs, and provided helpful criticism; Douglas H. Strong, who encouraged me to begin and who later read the manuscript and made valuable suggestions; photographers Jim Hildinger, Linda Anne Mainville, Eslie Cann, Philip Adam, and Robert McKimmie; artist Claus Sievert; Monica Clyde, Helmi Nock, and Hans Hollitscher for their translation of the Preuss diary from the German; Ted Inouye and Dick Reich of the US Geological Survey; Jim Ryan of the California Department of Fish and Game; and Lorene and Philip Greuner. I am grateful to the University of California Press for permission to use a few passages from the book *Up and Down California in 1860–1864, the Journal of William H. Brewer.* I also wish to thank the many helpful librarians at the Library of Congress Manuscript Division, the Bancroft Library, the California

State Library California Room, the California Historical Society Library, the Nevada Historical Society Library, Sonoma State University Library, the Sierra Club Colby Library, the Wells Fargo History Room, and the Marin County Library, Anne T. Kent California Room.

I invite the reader to send me additional information, which I will collect for an eventual second edition. Address your letters to the author in care of Great West Books, P.O. Box 1028, Lafayette, CA 94549.

Introduction

The Lake Tahoe Basin is officially designated as the land inside the ridgeline of the mountains encircling the lake. (See the reference map on page xviii.) Only the names within the Lake Tahoe Basin are included in this work. The source of the place names is the United States Geological Survey, which mapped, edited, and published the 7.5' quadrangle maps between 1955 and 1973. In 1976 the US Forest Service Geometric Service Center prepared the quad maps for the US Forest Service Lake Tahoe Basin Management Unit. I have used the Forest Service maps except for the *Caples Lake* quad, which had not been issued by the Forest Service at the time this project began.

Each entry contains the place name in bold type, the state and county, and the quadrangle map name or names in italics. Information on each place name was obtained from many varied sources. (In some instances it proved impossible to discover anything at all.) The citation source appears at the end of each segment of information. It includes the author's name and the page reference. When the author and/or page number is not known, only the title is given. Authors with more than one work cited in the book appear with the author's name followed by one word from the title of each book; for example, James, *Heroes*, and James, *Lake*. A list of the sources cited, excluding newspapers, appears in the Bibliography. Newspaper references are given at the end of the citations.

In a number of instances, where a feature is named for the original homesteader or other owner of the land, I have given the location of the land in terms of section, township, and range. Each section is one square mile. There are thirty-six sections in a township, which is the basic unit of reference. A township is a square—six sections on a side. Thus, if you see the following abbreviation: sec. 1, T. 11 N., R. 17 E., it stands for section 1, Township 11 North, Range 17 East. This is on the *Echo Lake* quadrangle. The range and township numbers are printed on the map borders, and every section is numbered. The homesteads and patents referred to are records of when that piece of land left control of the federal government. These records are preserved on microfilm in the "control document index" files of the General Land Office at the Bureau of Land Management on Cottage Way in Sacramento.

Lake Tahoe history has been made by Washoe Indians, explorers, trappers, settlers, road surveyors, ranchers, lumbermen, developers of the early tourist industry, entrepreneurs, scientists, naturalists, writers, and the present inhabitants, land developers, and conservationists. Tahoe place names have evolved from all of these varied and colorful groups.

Few people are aware of the Washoe heritage at Lake Tahoe, since so few Washoe names exist to remind us of their past presence. *Tallac* and *Tahoe* are the only two Washoe names in the Tahoe basin that are on present-day maps.

The earliest reports on the Washoe date from the mid-1800s. In 1954 Alfred Louis Kroeber wrote: "The Washo have been unduly neglected by students of the Indian. What little is on record concerning them makes it difficult to place them." Lake Tahoe was the center of the Washoe world, as it still is today.

In February 1844 Washoe Indians counseled John Charles Frémont against crossing the Sierra Nevada in the dead of winter. He chose to ignore their advice, and in the crossing many of the party's animals perished, and his men suffered from the lack of provisions and from the cold. On February 13 Frémont and his cartographer, Charles Preuss, climbed Red Lake Peak, and from its summit became the first white men known to have seen Lake Tahoe. Frémont referred to it only as a "mountain lake." Preuss, on the map of 1848, named it "L. Bonpland" after Aimé Jacques Alexandre Bonpland (1772–1858), a French botanist and companion of the Prussian explorer Alexander von Humboldt (1769–1859).

Eleven years later, William Henderson, El Dorado County surveyor, made the first recorded survey for a wagon road across the Sierra. During the summer of that year, Sherman Day and George H. Goddard conducted a second wagon-road survey, under the direction of State Surveyor General Seneca Hunt Marlette. The Whitney Survey visited the east side of Lake Tahoe in 1863, as did the California-Nevada state boundary survey.

After the roads were built and the Comstock Lode discovered, thousands of people traveled through the region. Inns and way stations for the accommodation of travelers sprang up, and ranches, dairies, and lumbermills were created to meet the demand for produce and building materials. Much of the early history of the Lake Tahoe region is concerned with the destruction of the forests and the shipping of vast quantities of timber to the Washoe mines.

The wealthy of California and Nevada built summer estates along Tahoe's shores. Resorts welcomed the many tourists who sought the high mountain air, the glorious scenery, and the renowned fishing. After the Second World War, Tahoe changed from a primarily summer resort area to one of year-round activity. Much has changed since 1844, but for those who hold it sacred, the lake is as precious as always.

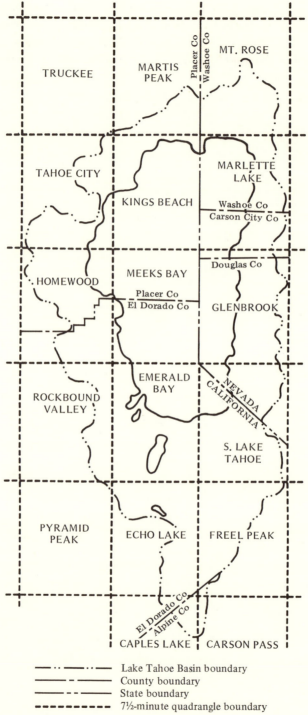

TRUCKEE

MARTIS PEAK

Placer Co | Washoe Co

MT. ROSE

TAHOE CITY

MARLETTE LAKE

KINGS BEACH

Washoe Co
Carson City Co

HOMEWOOD

MEEKS BAY

Douglas Co

Placer Co
El Dorado Co

GLENBROOK

ROCKBOUND VALLEY

EMERALD BAY

NEVADA
CALIFORNIA

S. LAKE TAHOE

PYRAMID PEAK

ECHO LAKE

FREEL PEAK

El Dorado Co
Alpine Co

CAPLES LAKE | CARSON PASS

— ·· — ·· — Lake Tahoe Basin boundary
— — — — County boundary
— — · — · State boundary
- - - - - - 7½-minute quadrangle boundary

Tahoe Place Names

Agate: Bay, Creek   California: Placer
Kings Beach

"It was near the end of May when our party got assembled and organized at the Wagner House, Lake Tahoe—pronounced *Ta-ho*—consisting of Houghton and Ives, Commissioners; Kidder and Lawson, Engineers; King, Crane, Bowman, Guilford and Fall of the line; Flynn, Brown, Wright, Bernardo and Domingo, of the camp and train. . . . Sails and oars may now be seen flying the waters of Lake Tahoe with all the energy of business." (*Sacramento Daily Union*, August 26, 1863. From the Eastern Boundary Survey.)

"**Progress of the Eastern Boundary Survey Expedition**. Since I wrote the *Bulletin* last, we have passed over some rough country. While camped at the foot of Lake Bigler, or Tahoe, as it is now often called, we had a very pleasant time. Our tent was pitched upon a small arm of the lake which we named Agate Bay, from the large number of agates found upon the beach." (*San Francisco Daily Evening Bulletin*, July 3, 1863.)

The name "Agate Bay" first appeared on the Ives, Houghton, and Kidder map, 1863. It is also on the von Leicht-Hoffmann map of 1874 and the Wheeler map of 1881.

Al Tahoe   California: El Dorado
South Lake Tahoe

The present-day community of Al Tahoe is the site of Lake Tahoe's first lakeshore hotel, the Lake House. "The proprietors of the . . . [Lake Valley House] . . . have within the past month completed a stable which will shelter one hundred and fifty horses, in addition to the stable accommodations previously occupied. This house is one of the largest in the country. Hundreds of men could be fed and lodged in it. The main building is built of logs, and for size they exceed any we ever saw put into a house. Their stand is about five miles north of Hawley's, and some two miles from the foot of the new grade from Johnson's Pass down into Lake Valley." (*Sacramento Daily Union*, November 16, 1860. See **Hawley Grade Trail** and **Johnson Pass**.)

In 1863 Brewer wrote: "We are camped in a pretty grove near the Lake House and a few rods from the lake. . . .

"The lake is *the* feature of the place. A large log hotel is here and many pleasure seekers are here, both from California and Nevada. . . .

"The purity of its waters, its great depth, its altitude, and the clear sky all combine to give the lake a bright but intensely blue color; it is bluer even than the Mediterranean. . . .

"The lake abounds in the largest trout in the world. . . . An Indian brought some into camp. I gave him fifty cents for two, and they made us two good meals and were excellent fish. He had speared them in a stream near. We were eating when he came; when we finished he wanted the remains, which I gave him. Rising satisfied, patting both hands on his stomach, he exclaimed, 'Belly goot—coot bye.' Many of these Indians, like the Chinese, cannot pronounce the letter R, substituting an L." (Brewer, *Up and Down*, 442–43.)

"**Inducements for Tourists**. The steamers being in running order, parties can go to any part of the lake without trouble. As for hotels, if one wishes to spend money freely, and be exceedingly fashionable, he can be accommodated at the Lake House, or at the Glenbrook Hotel; board $21 per week. If one wishes to have comfort, without much parade, there is the Logan House, board $15, or the Zephyr Cove House, board $12 per week. The fare from Sacramento, by the Pioneer Line, is $15, time eighteen hours; from Carson, $10, time six hours. From here there is a good road to the Big Trees, as one can go to Virginia [City] and back by way of Donner Lake, making one of the most interesting trips in the country. [signed] Stereoscope." (*San Francisco Daily Alta California*, July 1, 1865. See **Glenbrook**, **Logan Shoals**, and **Zephyr Cove**.)

Dan De Quille wrote: "Even the old Lake House, at Tahoe, though it was built of good pine logs and was very warm and substantial, has given way to more stylish structures. Times [1860s] are changed and few but pleasure-seekers are now seen on the old road where once the sounding 'blacksnake' awoke the echoes far and wide among the hills." (De Quille, *Bonanza*, 319.)

"Lake House" appeared on the Gibbes map of 1866, the year that it burned. Thomas B. Rowland bought the Lake House property in 1868, with thirty-three additional acres, and built another hotel. (Scott, 206.) The name "Lake Hs." appeared on the Hoffmann map of 1873.

On August 19, 1870 Joseph LeConte recorded in his *Ramblings Through the High Sierra*: "About 5 P. M. rode in double file up to Yank's and reined up. The fat, bluff old fellow cries out, 'Hello! where are you fellows from? Where are you going?' 'Excursion party to Tahoe; where best to stop?' 'You want to have a free, jolly time, don't you?' 'O, yes, certainly.' 'Well! you camp at this end of the lake, near Rowlands.'. . . We . . . camped at 7 P. M. in a fine grove of tamaracks, on the very borders of the lake."

The following day they hired a small sailboat. LeConte wrote: "Oh! the exquisite beauty of this lake—its clear waters, emerald-green, and the deepest ultramarine blue; its pure shores, rocky or cleanest gravel, so clean that the chafing of the waves does not stain in the least the bright clearness of the waters; the high granite mountains, with serried peaks, which stand close around its very shore to guard its crystal purity;—this lake, not *among*, but *on*, the mountains, lifted six thousand feet towards the deep-blue overarching sky, whose image it reflects! . . . We sailed some six or eight miles, and landed in a beautiful cove on the Nevada side." While sailing back they encountered very high winds and were later told by the owner of the boat that "*he* would not have risked the boat or his life in the middle of the lake on such a day." In closing, LeConte wrote: "I could dream away my life here with those I love. . . . Of all the places I have yet seen, this is the one which I could longest enjoy and love the most." (LeConte, *Ramblings*, 95–100.)

The name "Rowland's" appeared on the von Leicht-Hoffmann map of 1874. Tom Rowland's daughter, Fanny Rowland Barton, recalled the *Tahoe Tattler's* first editor and Tahoe's first photographer, R. E. Wood, stopping [in the 1880s] at Rowland's and presenting her with a bundle of his photographs of Tahoe scenery. "Many a pioneer's album [was] lined with his masterpieces." Rowland's dance hall and saloon collapsed in the winter snows of 1889–90. (*Tahoe Tattler*, August 30, 1935.)

Almerin R. Sprague built a hotel here in 1907 and named it partly for himself—the Al Tahoe Hotel. The community took its name from the hotel, and when a post office was established in 1908 Sprague became the first postmaster. (Salley, 5.) Scott mentions that the Al Tahoe Development Company tore down Rowland's old hotel, and "a six-room building adjoining the old landmark was sold to W. W. Price of Fallen Leaf Lodge, as was the over-water Custom House Saloon, which is now part of the main dining room at Fallen Leaf." (Scott, 209–10. See **Fallen Leaf Lake** and **Glen Alpine**.) James described the location of the modern, well-equipped lakeside hotel, with financial backing by Pasadena capitalists, "as one of the most beautiful spots of all this health giving region. Being of a lee shore, the cold air from the snowy summits of the mountains tempered by the warm soil of the foothills and level area, there is no place on the Lake better adapted for bathing and boating, especially as the beach is sandy and shallow, sloping off for some distance from the shore." (James, *Lake*, 230–31.)

Frank Globin bought the Al Tahoe Hotel in 1924, and added cabins and a casino. In the summer of 1938 the University of California Little Theatre launched the first summer theater in the West at Globin's Al Tahoe Chalet. The Mouse Trap Summer Theatre performed *All the World's a Stage* and *Goodbye Again*. Edwin Duerr, director of UC's Little Theatre, helped direct the productions. Globin housed the entire group, equipped the theater, and paid part of the production costs. (*Tahoe Tattler*, July 1, 15, and August 5, 12, 1938.)

"After forty-four years of operation, Globin's Al Tahoe resort was closed down in 1968." (Greuner, 34.)

Alta Morris Lake   California: El Dorado
Rockbound Valley

Origin unknown. The name first appeared on the 1945 Forest Service map.

Angora: Creek, Lakes, Lookout, Peak   California: El Dorado
Echo Lake
Emerald Bay

The Angora name is derived from a herd of Angora goats that Nathan Gilmore pastured in the region. (Sioli, 79.) "Angora Peak" appeared on the Wheeler map of 1881. James referred to the "Angora Range" and "Angora Lakes." (James, *Lake*, 84, 120.) The *Tahoe Tattler* for June 23, 1939 reported that Albert Wilhelm and Effie Hildinger were custodians at Angora Lakes. Forest Service records indicate the Hildinger family first leased the property in 1921–22. The Hildingers still operate a summer resort that offers cabin rentals and a snack bar to visiting hikers, swimmers, boaters, and picnickers. (Jim Hildinger. See **Gilmore Lake**.)

Antone Meadows   California: Placer
Tahoe City

Antone Russi, an early settler of Swiss extraction, bought Homer D. Burton's property, the island ranch near the lake shore, in the late 1880s. The 1874 von Leicht-Hoffmann map has the word "Island" at this location. Wheeler's 1881 map shows "Island House." Russi and his large family occupied Burton's old house, and Antone's name was given to the meadow where he pastured his cows. (Scott, 358. See **Burton Creek**.)

Balancing Rock.

Azure Lake   California: Placer
Emerald Bay
Rockbound Valley

Harry Oswald Comstock named the lake "Gladys" for one of his daughters. The lake's name was later changed to "Azure." (Eden.) That name appeared on the *Fallen Leaf Lake* 15-minute quad, 1958. A 1945 Forest Service map identified the lake as "Kalmeia Lake," and the present Kalmia Lake was not named. (See **Kalmia Lake** and **Velma Lakes**.)

Balancing Rock   California: Placer
Meeks Bay

This large granite rock, balanced on a much smaller base, is located in the D. L. Bliss State Park. "Whale's Head Rock" was the name used in a *Tahoe Tattler* article on June 28, 1935, which mentioned that the rock had appeared in Robert Ripley's "Believe it or Not" feature. (See **D. L. Bliss State Park** and **Bliss Creek**.)

Baldwin Beach   California: El Dorado
Emerald Bay

Baldwin Beach once belonged to a Virginia City miner, E. J. "Lucky" Baldwin, who in 1890 bought Ephraim "Yank" Clement's hotel, built in 1875. (See **Meyers** and **Tallac**.) By 1926 Baldwin had amassed 2,647 acres, including one mile of beach. His Hotel Tallac was known throughout the West for its excellent accommodations, its proximity to the lake, and for the beauty of the mountain scenery. "Gulls, pelicans and mud hens can generally be seen in large numbers around the piers at Tallac, and the fleet of fishing boats, each with its one or more eager anglers, is one of the sights." (James, *Lake*, 209.) "Baldwin was a great lover of trees, and when the present hotel and cottages were built, not a single tree was cut without his express permission." (James, *Lake*, 208.)

"Lucky Baldwin owns the wooded lands lying contiguous. With a high consideration which bespeaks him a man and not a mere money bag, he has consecrated those forests and groves to their own perpetual beauty. He has declared they shall never be surrendered to the woodsman's ax. He stands by Nature as her one firm, effectual friend." (Mighels, 173.)

"More than anyone else, Ray Knisley was responsible for the conversion of lands around Baldwin Beach, Fallen Leaf Lake, Camp Richardson and Pope Beach from private to public use." (Bixler, 100.

See **Fallen Leaf Lake, Camp Richardson,** and **Pope Beach**.) The US Forest Service purchased the Baldwin estate, including its beaches, in 1950 and 1951. (Strong, 83.)

Baldy, Mount   Nevada: Washoe
Mount Rose
   A descriptive name for a mountain that appears relatively devoid of vegetation. (Carlson, 45.)

Barker Peak   California: Placer
Homewood
   Rancher William Andrew Barker held "the finest grazing land in the High Sierra." (Scott, 64.) The name appeared as "Bawker's Peak" on the von Leicht-Hoffmann map of 1874, and as "Barker's Peak" on Wheeler's 1881 map.

Becker Peak   California: El Dorado
Echo Lake
   The peak is named for John S. Becker, who in 1886 built a cabin "near the lower end of Lower Echo Lake and gradually expanded until

Courtesy, Nevada Historical Society

Washoe in camp near Lakeside Park, Lake Tahoe.

he was running in connection with his cattle ranch a first class saloon, the mecca of holiday-minded folk who traveled the old Pony Express route." (*Tahoe Tattler*, August 13, 1937.) Becker officially homesteaded five lots in the northern part of sec. 1, T. 11 N., R. 17 E. on April 8, 1904. "Becker Peak" appeared on the 1958 *Fallen Leaf Lake* 15-minute quad, but not on the Forest Service 1945 map.

Benwood Meadow   California: El Dorado
Echo Lake
   Origin unknown. The name appeared on the 1958 *Fallen Leaf Lake* 15-minute quad, but not on the Forest Service 1945 map.

Big Meadow; Big Meadow Creek   California: El Dorado
Echo Lake
Freel Peak
   These are obvious descriptive names, but their origin is unknown. They appeared on the 1958 *Fallen Leaf Lake* 15-minute quad, but were not on the 1945 Forest Service map.

Bijou   California: El Dorado
South Lake Tahoe
   Washoe Indian archeological findings here include grinding stones and evidence of a major trail leading south and east into Carson Valley. (Freed, *Washo*, 82.)
   Captain Almon M. (Jim) Taylor patented 157.49 acres in sec. 33, T. 13 N., R. 18 E. on December 18, 1864. In 1862 he had leased grass-cutting rights. In the 1870s "Taylor's Landing" was the terminus for George Washington Chubbuck's tramline railroad. A pier was built and railroad tracks were laid in 1888 as lumbering surged to 21,000,000 board feet. (Scott, 215.) The name "J. Taylor" appeared on the von Leicht-Hoffmann map of 1874.
   The post office at Rowland's moved to Taylor's Landing, and officially became known as "Bijou" on September 11, 1888. (Salley, 21.) *Bijou*, a French word meaning "gem," "jewel," "treasure," was applied to the settlement of Taylor's Landing during the late 1880s by French Canadian lumberjacks, or by William S. Bliss (son of D. L. Bliss) and Cary Platt, who jointly decided upon the name, or by "Bonnie" Oakley, a Bijou school teacher. (Scott, 211.)
   The name "Bijou" appeared on the first *Markleeville* 30-minute map, 1891.

James described a Bijou resort named Camp Bell, managed by Russell W. Bell, as consisting "of tents and an open-air dining room. . . . Bijou Inn on the Lake Shore Drive near to the State Highway and close to Freel's and the other mountain peaks of this group. The beach in front of Bijou is of clean white sand, with a gentle slope, offering excellent facilities for bathing." Lakeside Park was where "Patrons of the hotel or camps are assured that there are no rattlesnakes, fleas, malaria, fogs, or poison oak. The character and tone of the place will also be recognized when it is known that saloons and gambling resorts are absolutely prohibited in the residential tract." (James, *Lake*, 384, 252.)

Blackwood: Creek, Ridge   California: Placer
Homewood

One of the principal trout-spawning creeks of Lake Tahoe, Blackwood Creek was named for a fisherman and early settler, Hampton Craig Blackwood. Blackwood was a native of North Carolina, a miner, and a resident of Mud Springs in 1866. Sometime after July 1866 he settled at the mouth of the creek that bears his name. (*Great Register.*) "Blackwood Pass," a trail at the head of Blackwood Creek and outside the Lake Tahoe Basin, is in the Wheeler Survey report of 1876–77 and on the map of 1881.

Freed reports that the Washoe Indians camped "on the south side of a small hill just north of the creek." Among other activities, the Washoe trapped "ground squirrels and woodchucks, and gathered porcupine berries and wild rhubarb. Cutthroat trout ran here early in the spring and were then followed by other fish." (Freed, *Washo*, 81.)

Bliss Creek   Nevada: Carson City
Marlette Lake

The creek is probably named for Duane Leroy Bliss, who with Henry Marvin Yerington started the Carson & Tahoe Lumber and Fluming Company, which incorporated and moved to Glenbrook in 1873. Bliss built railroads, cut down most of Tahoe's timberlands, bought the Glenbrook Hotel, and were the owners and builders of the 200-passenger steamer *Tahoe*, the "Queen of the Lake." The Carson and Tahoe Lumber and Fluming Company is thought to have logged as much as 750,000,000 board feet of lumber and 500,000 cords of wood in a period of twenty-eight years. (Shinn, 116–18.) In the words of Dan De Quille, "The Comstock lode may truthfully be said to be the tomb of the forests of the Sierras. Other large mills besides those of the company named are engaged in devouring the forest surrounding Lake

Tahoe. About five million feet of lumber per month are turned out by the several mills at the lake, and each summer about three million feet of timbers are hewn in that locality." (De Quille, *Bonanza*, 174, 178. See **D. L. Bliss State Park** and **Duane Bliss Peak**.)

Brockway (Community)   California: Placer
Brockway: Spring, Summit
Kings Beach
Martis Peak

A newspaper correspondent signing himself "The Mountaineer" reported from Lake Tahoe: "Hot springs. . . There are at the north end of the lake, hot chalybiate springs. These springs are located on the shore of the lake, extending along the same to the distance of perhaps a hundred yards, and into the lake, in some places, more than one hundred feet, forming one of the finest natural mineral baths in the world. At a comparatively trifling expense, baths and other accommodations could be provided here to meet the wishes of the most fastidious. This point must necessarily become, very soon, a second Bethesda, particularly with those who are induced to spend most of their time in sections where the air is rarified, the dust impregnated with alkali, or the waters with arsinic [*sic*]; to them chalybiates are indispensable." (*Sacramento Daily Union*, December 9, 1863.)

Hoffmann noted the name "Warm Springs" on the 1873 map. "Hot Springs Hotel" appeared on the von Leicht-Hoffmann map of 1874, and "Warm Springs" on the *Map of the Comstock Area* in 1875. "The Hot Springs Hotel was so full recently that I was compelled to spread myself in a small upper chamber, in immediate contiguity to the roof. R. A. Ricker has charge of the Hot Springs Hotel this year, as last, and is making it one of the most popular resorts on the lake. He is about to furnish a number of family cottages; he will, therefore, soon have increased room." (*San Francisco Daily Evening Bulletin*, July 15, 1873.) The resort had boiling soda and sulphur water in the bath house, hot water in the rooms, and pleasant accommodations. Guests were advised to bring their mountain clothes, because this was "not a dressy place." (Talbot.) A post office opened March 16, 1901 and was named "Brockway" for Frank Brockway Alverson's uncle, Nathaniel Brockway. Alverson was its first postmaster. (Salley, 27.) The community took its name from the hot-springs resort, Brockways, owned and operated by F. B. Alverson. (James, *Lake*, 384.)

Buck Lake   California: Placer

Homewood

Buck, Bear, Duck, and Quail lakes lie in the vicinity of Ellis Peak, and within fair distance of the old-time favorite, McKinney's Hunter's Retreat on McKinney Bay. These common names were probably given by hunters from McKinney's. (See **McKinney**.)

Burke Creek   Nevada: Douglas

South Lake Tahoe

A bedrock mortar site along the creek indicates that Washoes frequented the area. (Freed, *Washo*, 82.)

In March of 1860 Martin K. "Friday" Burke and James "Jim" Washington Small preempted 320 acres near the southeast shore of Lake Tahoe, where they built a log cabin along an improved Washoe Indian game path that wound north along the lakeshore toward Cave Rock. (Scott, 231. See **Cave Rock**.)

Burke started the first commercial fishing business, known as Burke & Company. (*Sacramento Daily Union*, September 6, 1862.) Together with J. W. Small he operated Burke and Small's Station. "A correspondent of the Virginia *Union*, writing from Lake Valley, gives an array of facts which show a most wanton and unreasonable destruction of this valuable fish. He says one firm has been plying its vocation for some three years and have a seine six hundred yards long, to which are attached gill net wings as much longer, thus sweeping over the spawn beds of the trout and taking occasionally a thousand pounds per night. Millions of eggs, too, are thus destroyed. These nets are dragged only in the spawning season. Another company has miles of gill nets, but no seine. These two companies catch about eighteen tons of trout during the year." (*Sacramento Daily Union*, June 23, 1864.)

On the Wheeler map of 1881, surveyed in 1876 and 1877, the creek is called "Friday Cr." and the station, "Small's." In 1860 Friday's Station became a Pony Express "home station" and a Wells Fargo and Pioneer Stage Lines station along the Johnson Pass-Kingsbury trail between California and Nevada. (Bloss, 62, 99; Scott, 232.) The von Leicht-Hoffmann map of 1874 showed "Friday's." In 1888 John Wales Averill bought the property and named it "Edgewood." In 1897 Averill's widow sold the property to David Brooks Park of Mottsville, Nevada, whose son, David Wallace Park, tore down the Wells Fargo and Pioneer Stage Lines' barn, which had been one of the largest barns in the west. Still in existence are the original house with its ridgepole, rafters, and hand-hewn interior walls and floor, and one log cabin that served as a blacksmith shop. (Scott, 237.)

Burton Creek   California: Placer
Kings Beach
Tahoe City

The creek was named for Captain Homer D. Burton, "who has lived on the lake for more than thirty years, and drove the first wagon team that ever came to the lake, camping that night at Glenbrook." The Captain told fish stories about having caught the largest trout ever, 29¾ pounds, which he sent to President Grant for Christmas dinner. The president sent a letter acknowledging receipt of the fish. (*Sacramento Daily Union*, June 15, 1890.)

On October 25, 1871 Burton homesteaded 142 acres in sec. 32, T. 16 N., R. 17 E., and sec. 4, T. 15 N., R. 17 E., and on March 5, 1880 he homesteaded additional land in sec. 32, T. 16 N., R. 17 E. James mentioned that Burton had been a Squaw Valley miner. "When the 'bottom fell out' of that he did a variety of things to earn a living, one of which was to cut bunch grass from Lake Valley, and bring it on mules over the pass that bears his name, boat it across to Lakeside at the south end of the Lake, on the Placerville and Virginia City stage-road, and there sell it to the stage station. Hay thus gathered was worth in those days from $80 to $100 per ton." (James, *Lake*, 154–55.) The name "Burton Pass" appeared on the Hoffmann map of 1873. The name "Island" appeared on the von Leicht-Hoffmann map of 1874. The Wheeler map of 1881 showed "Island House." (See **Antone Meadows**.) Washoe Indians called this camp *wO'thanamIn* (*wO'tha* means "river"). "Whitefish were taken in this creek and grasshoppers were collected in nearby meadows. . . . Big green worms (probably army worms) that live on trees were collected and roasted in hot sand." (Freed. *Washo*, 81.)

Cagwin Lake   California: El Dorado
Echo Lake

A lake above Upper Echo Lake was named for the "Hermit of the Lake," Hamden El Dorado Cagwin, a skillful hunter and fisherman, who settled at Lower Echo Lake in 1896. Cagwin was only four years old when he and his mother arrived in California via the hazardous Isthmus route, and joined Cagwin's father in Hangtown. Years later he inherited a stationery shop, but after two years sold it to his brother. He went to Oregon, Washington, Carson City, and Hope Valley before he built a cabin on the north side of Lower Echo Lake, and served as guide and caretaker of the El Dorado Gravel and Deep Water Mining Company dam and flume. Like Snowshoe Thompson, Cagwin was a skilled snowshoer; he carried mail from Strawberry Valley to Carson City, and helped in emergencies. In 1916 a party of Washoes fishing at Echo Lake discovered his body in his cabin. (*Tahoe Tattler*, August 13, 1937.)

California

The name of this glorious state is probably derived from a fifteenth century Spanish novel about "an island called California, very close to that part of the Terrestrial Paradise. . . ." California "was ruled by a queen, Calafia, of majestic proportions, more beautiful than all the others. . . ." (Putnam, 306.)

The American author and educator George Tichnor is credited with pointing out this coincidence in 1849. (Davidson, 21.) The word "California" first appears in Montalvo's novel *Las sergas del muy esforzado caballero Esplandian, hijo del excelente rey Amadis de Gaula* (The exploits of the very valiant knight Esplandian, son of the excellent king Amadis of Gaul) that he wrote as a sequel to the Portugese novel *Amadis de Gaula*, which he had translated in the late 1490s.

"Chapter 157, containing that portion describing the golden island of California, was published in the original Spanish with English translation, in the Sixth Annual Report of the State Mineralogist of California, folio 8." (*San Francisco Mining and Scientific Press*, November 17, 1888.)

The name "California" later was applied to the land discovered by Spanish explorers. Juan Rodríguez Cabrillo used the name three times in the journal of his voyage in 1542. The name appeared on a map by Diego Guitérrez in 1562. (Putnam, 349.)

Camp Harvey West   California: El Dorado
Echo Lake

Lumberman Harvey West grew up in Santa Cruz County, where his Canadian-born father logged redwoods. West later moved to El Dorado County and built sawmills at Placerville, Kyburz, Fresh Pond, and Tahoe Valley. West donated $45,000 to the Boy Scouts of America to build one of the finest scout camps in the nation. On July 23, 1950 he dedicated the camp in memory of his father, James E. West, "For the Purpose of Character Building Through Outdoor Adventures."

West is remembered for his generosity, and perhaps for these words of wisdom: "Do not regret growing old. It is a privilege denied to many." (Bixler, 171–72.)

Camp Richardson
California: El Dorado
Emerald Bay

Washoe Indians camped in an area between Taylor and Tallac creeks "on the first stream west of Camp Richardson." Its name was *daugacacuwO'tha*, which translates as "clear water river." Freed suggests that the place "was visited from spring to the middle of summer. The Washo caught spotted trout in the river and collected birds' eggs in a nearby swamp." (Freed, *Washo*, 78, 80.)

Matthew Gardner built a standard-gauge railroad in 1875 while working for the Carson Tahoe Lumber and Fluming Co. (Strong, 27. See **Gardner Mountain**.) Al "Rich" Richardson bought the Lawrence and Comstock holdings in 1923. He put up tourist cabins, built a pier, and in 1927 had the post office transferred from the Tallac Hotel. He also operated a motor stage line between Tallac and Sacramento. (Bixler, 99.) James mentioned a "Richardson Peak" in the vicinity of Glen Alpine, but this name does not now appear. (James, *Lake*, 237.) In 1974 the Camp Richardson property was acquired by the US Forest Service in exchange for summer home tracts at Cedar Flat and Al Tahoe. (Greuner, 42.) The resort is still in operation.

Camp Wasiu
California: Placer
Homewood

Located near Meeks Creek above Meeks Bay. *Wasiu* and *Wa sui* are perhaps variations of the Indian tribe name *Washo*. (Davis, *Nevada*, 26.)

Caples Lake Quadrangle
California: El Dorado, Alpine

Dr. Caples of Sacramento brought 6,000 head of sheep up to Summit Lakes. (*Alpine Chronicle* (Silver Mountain), June 12, 1869.) "'Caple's Lake' is located just west of the summit in the El Dorado National Forest, which is in the vicinity of the doctor's old grazing area." (Maule, 45.)

Dr. James Caples was born in Tuscarawas County, Ohio on November 29, 1823. When he was fourteen his family moved to Andrew County, Missouri. At nineteen years he studied medicine under his father's youngest brother, Jacob. In 1847 he moved to Hancock County, Illinois and practiced medicine for two years, during which time he married Mary Jane Walker. On March 21, 1849, with a wagon and three yoke of oxen, they joined a company bound for California. Along the way Caples "lost his senses" from drinking bad water. On the ascent of Carson Canyon Mrs. Caples walked and carried their infant in her arms. A few days after they arrived in Hangtown on August 28, 1849,

Dr. Caples purchased a little store, but sold it to enter the mining business. He nearly succumbed to dysentery and was saved from death by his medical knowledge and the care of his wife. He regained his strength by drinking milk and then eating only rice. Once again he purchased a small store, and enlarged his holdings to control all the mercantile business in Hangtown. Later he purchased a ranch, and increased his land holdings to some 4,000 acres at the junction of Deer and Carson creeks. He was successful in raising horses and sheep, but not cattle. In 1882 he moved to a ranch on the Cosumnes River three miles from Elk Grove. He served at the State Constitutional Convention of 1879, and was the father of nine children. (Davis, *Sacramento*, 700–702.)

Courtesy, California Historical Society, San Francisco

Joseph and Ernest John Pomin, about 1910.

Originally there were two small lakes, known as "Twin Lakes." Pacific Gas and Electric dammed the creek, creating the present larger lake. The "Caples" name was given to the lake and the creek in honor and memory of early pioneers, the Caples family.

Captain Pomin Rock   Nevada: Douglas
Glenbrook

William Pomin was one of the first settlers at Lake Tahoe. His daughter was the first white child born at the lake. The rock appears to have been named for his brother Ernest John, who was captain of the steamer *Tahoe*. Captain Ernest John Pomin was a "nice gentleman and a good sailor," who knew every rock and shoal on Lake Tahoe. (Scott, 405.) He died accidentally on December 8, 1919 at the age of seventy-one after forty-five years of dedicated service to the Bliss Family. (Scott, 432.)

The rock, which is 7,538 feet in elevation, is due east and directly above Glenbrook Bay and the community of Glenbrook.

Carnelian Bay   California: Placer
Kings Beach

The name was originally spelled "Cornelian."

"A Cruise On A Mountain Sea. Number Four. . . . When the voyagers embarked [on the schooner *El Dorado*] next morning, the lake opposite Tahoe City was smooth, shining and breathless. There had been a lively desire to explore Cornelian Bay, to examine the Hot Springs on the northern shore and to take a near view of Cave Rock on the eastern shore. . . . Upon leaving the landing, such a dead calm prevailed that, in order to make any headway, it was necessary to put out the oars and take a good sweat at the manly exercise of rowing." (*Sacramento Daily Union*, August 4, 1866.)

"After a ride of some two hours duration, through the noble pine forests which border the lake, we reached Cornelian Bay, (so called from the number of Cornelian stones found there), and immediately distributed ourselves along the beach, rooting for pebbles, and with good success, for at the end of an hour, we had each obtained a pocketful of beautiful specimens." (*San Francisco Daily Alta California*, August 22, 1870.)

The name "Cornelian" is shown on the von Leicht-Hoffmann map of 1874 and the Wheeler map of 1881. Alfred R. Conkling used the name "Cornelian Bay" in his report to Wheeler for the field season of 1876. (Wheeler, *Report*, 1291.)

"There are several small villages on the shore of the lake; there are some Hot Springs; there is Cornelian Beach, where tiny red and yellow cornelians can be picked up by handfuls. . . ." (Jackson, 152.)

"Mrs. Wood, of Carnelian Bay, was out star gazing last evening, when a magnificent meteor shot from the north east out over the lake, and burst with a loud report, sending off many different colored scintillations similar to a first-class rocket." (*Tahoe Tattler*, July 28, 1881.) The post office dates from 1883. (Salley, 38.)

The von Leicht-Hoffmann map included the name "Kuhleborn" for a trail leading away from Carnelian Bay toward a lake below Mt. Pluto. An ethnographic site was located at Watson Creek where it empties into the Lake. The suggested meaning of the name *masundauwO'tha* is "slow river." "The camp site on Watson Creek was back a short distance from the lake. This was an important camping ground for the Indians from around Carson City and Reno, who might spend the whole summer here. Besides fishing, the Washo hunted ground squirrels and woodchucks, and gathered several kinds of seeds (*mA'sum*, pigweed seed, *cugIlatsi*, and *sEsmE'*). They also collected mushrooms, locusts, and a kind of berry called *k!ila'tsim*." (Freed, *Washo*, 81–82. See **Watson**.)

Carson City County   Nevada
Carson City

Carson City County was originally named Ormsby County, which was created by an act of the Territorial Legislature, and approved November 25, 1861. (See **Ormsby**.) The county's name was officially changed in 1969 after the city and county consolidated.

Carson City and the Carson River were named for Christopher "Kit" Carson by John C. Frémont. (Davis, *Nevada*, 21.) Carson's name is "applied to the beautiful river that first greets the thirsty traveler from the East and points the way to the crossing of the Sierra. . . ." (Angel, *Nevada*, 528.)

Carson was born December 24, 1809 in Madison County, Kentucky. In his first year his family moved to Howard County, Missouri and lived near Fort Hempstead. At age fifteen Carson was apprenticed to a saddlemaker. Two years later, "being anxious to travel for the purpose of seeing different countries, [Carson] concluded to join the first party that started for the Rocky Mountains." Thus began Carson's career as an adventurer and guide, and his eventual transformation into an American folk hero. (Carson, 3–5.)

Kit Carson.

Cascade: Creek, Lake   California: El Dorado
Emerald Bay

    Lieutenant M. M. Macomb reported in 1877 that "Cascade Lake (300 feet above Tahoe) is oval in shape, and about a mile long, deriving its name from a fine water-fall some 250 feet high at its head." (Wheeler, *Report*, 1281.) The glacial origins of the lakes in this region are described in Professors John and Joseph LeConte's geologic reports. "I have never anywhere seen more perfectly defined moraines. I climbed over the larger western moraine and found that it is partly merged into the eastern moraine of Emerald Bay to form a medial at least 300 feet high, and of great breadth. From the surface of the little lake the curving branches of the main moraine, meeting below the lake to form a terminal moraine, are very distinct." (LeConte, *Glacier*, 129.)

Freed lists this area as an ethnographic site where the Washo "occasionally caught *Cui-ui*. They called the place *dEyEli'bukhwOnhu* (meaning unknown), but it was not a specially popular camping spot. (Freed, *Washo*, 80.)

"One of the most entertaining characters about here is 'Jimmy Walker,' who has lived a hermit life in a little cabin on the lake shore in a pretty spot where the stream from Cascade Lake empties into Tahoe. Jimmy has lived alone in that one cabin, winter and summer, for eleven years, but relaxes the severity of this hermitage in the summer to the extent of entertaining at lunch favored tourists who have discovered that he is the only man within miles who can cook a trout decently." (*San Francisco Morning Call*, July 15, 1883.)

Dr. Charles Brooks Brigham bought the property east of Cascade Lake in the spring of 1882, and later increased the size of his holdings. Both Mark Twain and John Muir were guests of the Brighams. (Scott, 139.) On a trip with botanist Charles C. Parry, Muir described his visit to Cascade Lake on July 1, 1888: "Snowy mountains and a fall and a grand glacier basin, and well-timbered lateral moraines, make a fine setting for Cascade Lake. I saw a duck with her young sailing and running on the lake, a fine, wild, happy sight. Also young robins and young grouse . . . . Landed at Dr. Brigham's cottage, bark-covered, neatly shingled, with wide verandahs. Flakes of bark on the sides in handsome patterns . . . very tastefully rustic. . . ." (Wolfe, 287.)

In 1897 Brigham gave property northwest of the lake to his brother-in-law. Much of the property was given to the California State Park System by Dr. Brigham's youngest daughter, Katherine Brigham Ebright, and her sons Charles and Harry. (Scott, 139–42.)

The movie *Lightnin'* starring Will Rogers was shot at Cascade Lake. It depicts Frank Bacon, a California-Nevada Stateline character. (*Tahoe Tattler*, August 23, 1935.) The film *Rose Marie* starring Jeannette McDonald and Nelson Eddy was filmed at Carnelian Bay, Emerald Bay, and Cascade Lake in the Rubicon area. Hundreds of Indians were recruited from the Carson Indian School as extras for the film. (*Tahoe Tattler*, December 20, 1935. See **Carnelian Bay** and **Emerald Bay**.)

Courtesy, California Historical Society, San Francisco
The Land of the Totem Poles, recreated at Cascade Lake
in 1936 for the movie *Rose Marie*. Photo by Ted Huggins.

Castle Rock   California: El Dorado
South Lake Tahoe

Origin unknown; a commonplace name. Castle Rock is a peak 1.5
miles northwest of Daggett Pass. There are nineteen places or forma-
tions in California named "Castle Rock." Seven of them are summits,
eight are pillars, and four are islands. (See **Daggett Pass**.)

Cathedral: Creek, Lake, Peak   California: El Dorado
Emerald Bay

According to James there were two Cathedral Peaks at Lake Tahoe,
"one above Cathedral Park at Fallen Leaf Lake, the other at the rear of
Emerald Bay Camp." Carl Fluegge, an expert guide and huntsman,
opened the Cathedral Park resort on the west side of Fallen Leaf Lake
in 1912. Mrs. Fluegge guaranteed the ladies the best of care. (James,
Lake, 227, 247–50.)

"The shortest route up Tallac, the Cathedral Trail is probably the steepest tract in the Wilderness, climbing 3355' in 4.4 miles. . . . Cathedral Peak . . . is actually the nose of Tallac's southeast ridge, although from Fallen Leaf it appears to be a formidable mountain." (Wood, 235–37. See **Fallen Leaf** and **Tallac**.)

Cave Rock   Nevada: Douglas
Glenbrook

Lt. M. M. Macomb reported that "The rock derives its name from a cave extending some 30 feet into its side." (Wheeler, *Report*, 1280.) Freed suggested that the Washoe Indian name is *dE'Ekwadapoc*, meaning "gray rock." "The cave at Cave Rock was used as a shelter. About one hundred yards offshore from this rock was the nest of a mythical man-eating bird ('an)." (Freed, *Washo*, 82.)

". . . Under a rocky point on the east shore of the lake, is the celebrated Indian cave, with its legendary romance. . . .

"But our poor attempt of the pencil can give but a faint idea of the beauty of the spot; we can only hope to recall to those, whose eye has already beheld the scene, what must ever be, one of memory's most pleasing pictures; while in those who have not yet seen it we hope to induce a desire to visit one of California's noblest lakes." (Goddard, *Bigler*, 108–9.)

The first use of the name "Cave Rock" on a map is on Lawson and Ives' *Township Lines*, 1861.

"We now take a nearer look at Cave Rock from the road, at Sierra Rocks, and also have a fine view of Rocky Point. Nothing can be more beautiful than the view from this position. The road comes to the edge of the lake; it is well watered, smooth, and has running water every half mile. We next come to the Cave Rock, where there is a fine, smooth and broad road, leading around its base, at some distance above the water, while above us rises a perpendicular mass of rock to the height of two hundred feet, and on the summit stands a lofty flag-pole, from which floated proudly our glorious flag, until some dastardly wretch, to whom it was a reproach for his treason, vented his spite by cutting the ropes and destroying the flag. Here one can obtain a fine view of the lake, being able to see almost the whole of that noble sheet of water. The summits on the western shore loom up grandly, and the waves dashing musically at our feet. You clamber up into the cave; the entrance is grand, but the cave continues only a short distance, and on its walls is a kind of pitch or resin which is black and has a bitter but not disagreeable taste. In ascending the rock and near the summit, you encounter huge, broken rocks, but a passage is found through them, and the traveller soon arrives on the summit, and stands at the base of the flag-pole. Here a view meets the eye that cannot be surpassed by any on this coast, and it is conceded by all, that for beauty and grandeur the views on this coast cannot be excelled. . . . [signed] Stereoscope." (*San Francisco Daily Alta California*, July 1, 1865.)

"Cave Rock" appeared on the von Leicht-Hoffmann map of 1874 and the Wheeler map of 1881. The rock was described by Lt. M. M. Macomb in 1876 as a prominent "mass of porphyritic trachyte rising some 150 feet above the lake, the road being carried around its base on trestle-work." (Wheeler, *Report*, 1280.) Highway 50 now passes through the rock formation.

Courtesy, Southern Pacific Company

Cave Rock, when the road went around it rather than through it as it does now.

Cedar Flat   California: Placer
Kings Beach

The namer is unknown, but it is an obvious descriptive name deriv-
ing from the incense cedar (*Libocedrus decurrens*).

Chambers Lodge   California: Placer
Homewood

In 1920 David Henry Chambers bought McKinney's resort and renamed it "Chambers' Lodge." McKinney's Hunter's Retreat had been
established in 1861 or 1863 by John Washington McKinney. (See **Mc-
Kinney**.) "The main part of the commodious hotel is built from rare
sugar-pine, which was transported from the other side of the Lake."
(MacDonald, 19.) The Chambers Lodge post office opened November
1, 1928, and was discontinued March 31, 1959. (Salley, 41.)

China Gardens   Nevada: Douglas
Glenbrook

Chinese "cordwood cutters, splitters and loaders; engineers,
firemen, brakemen, oilers, teamsters, swampers, flumesmen, mules-
kinners, blacksmiths, foremen and cooks" worked at Glenbrook and
Bijou in the 1890s. (Scott, 270, 216.) The Chinese grew vegetables in the
Glenbrook meadow, which was the original Chinese Gardens. (Scott,
491.) Lower Prey Meadows also was known as "Chinese Gardens" at
one time. The present "China Gardens" is situated near Glenbrook Bay
at the entrance to Slaughterhouse Canyon. (See **Glenbrook, Bijou,
Lower Prey Meadows,** and **Slaughterhouse Canyon**.)

Christopher, Lake   California: El Dorado
South Lake Tahoe

Origin unknown. The lake was created by damming Trout Creek.
(See **Trout Creek**.)

Cliff Lake   California: El Dorado
Rockbound Valley

Origin unknown, but it is an obvious name. The lake has cliffs all
around except at its outlet, to the north. The name appeared on the
1945 Forest Service map and on the 1958 *Fallen Leaf Lake* 15-minute
quad.

Cold Creek   California: El Dorado
South Lake Tahoe

In the summer of 1859 Robert Garwood Dean established the Sierra House in a meadow overlooking a small stream—Cold Creek. (*Sacramento Daily Union*, November 16, 1860. See **Sierra House**.) "Cold Creek" appeared on the Wheeler map of 1881 and the first *Dardanelles* 30-minute map, 1898.

Cracked Crag   California: El Dorado
Pyramid Peak

The word "crag" is of Celtic origin, perhaps with the basic meaning of "to hang suspended." (Partridge, 127.) It is often used to describe a broken cliff or naked spur like the sheer broken mountain ledge above Lake Aloha (not in the Tahoe Basin), which was formerly known as "Medley Lakes." (Wood, 79.) The name appeared on the 1958 *Fallen Leaf Lake* 15-minute quad but not on the 1945 Forest Service map.

Crag Lake   California: El Dorado
Rockbound Valley

An obvious descriptive name for a lake surrounded by crags. The name appeared on both the 1945 Forest Service map and on the *Fallen Leaf Lake* 15-minute quad, 1958.

Crystal Bay   Nevada: Washoe; California: Placer
Marlette Lake
Kings Beach

The bay may have been named for George Iweis Crystal who filed with the General Land Office for land on the north shore of Lake Tahoe. (Scott, 317.) Another possible explanation might be the "very pretty collection of crystals, mica and pieces called petrified wood from Crystal Bay . . . ." (*Tahoe Tattler*, October 22, 1881.) "Crystal B." appeared on the Hoffmann map of 1873, on the von Leicht-Hoffmann map of 1874, and on the Wheeler map of 1881. In 1876 Alfred R. Conkling referred to an earlier name, "Todman Bay," for Captain Joseph A. Todman of Glenbrook. (Wheeler, *Report*, 1289, 1291.) John Muir made camp "at an old log-slide on the east side of a rocky point on the west shore of Crystal Bay. Just enough sand to sleep between boulders. Had a good fire, and a good bed of dwarf oak and Vaccinifolium, *Quercus vaccinifolia*." (Wolfe, 288.)

D. L. Bliss State Park   California: El Dorado
Meeks Bay

In June 1928 William, Walter, and Hope Bliss offered to donate land to the state of California for a park to be named in memory of their father, Duane L. Bliss, Jr. (Gudde, 31; Strong, 86.) "Immediately after voter approval of the matching funds, the State Park Commission under William E. Colby approved Rubicon Point as the first project on which state bond money would be spent. After four years of negotiations, the state acquired more than nine hundred acres of scenic land, including 14,840 feet of Tahoe lakeshore and 3,500 feet on Emerald Bay, valued at $265,000, half of which was generously donated by the Bliss family." (Strong, 86. See **Duane Bliss Peak.**)

Daggett: Creek, Pass
South Fork Daggett Creek   Nevada: Douglas
South Lake Tahoe

El Dorado County surveyor William Henderson noted the origin of the name for the pass and the creek on February 23, 1855, when he traveled up to Tahoe and over to Dr. Daggett's with Messrs. Taylor and Silman. "Thence south sixty-four degrees, east three miles and four chains brought us to Dr. Daggett's, at the foot of the mountain and on the west side of Carson Valley, making the whole distance from Placerville to this place sixty-four and three-eighths miles." (Henderson, 9.)

George H. Goddard recorded on September 6, 1855: "We traveled along but slowly. On reaching Dr. Daggett's we received a hearty welcome, and he produced from his garden some very fine musk and water melons, which was a treat to us after our mountain fare." (Goddard, *Report*, 107.) Sherman Day, on the same survey with Goddard, reported on September 20, 1855: "There is a pass in the rear of Dr. Daggett's, about three miles south of the Mormon Station, leading to the south-east corner of Lake Bigler, but it is only used for horses and mules, having never been graded for wagons." (Goddard, *Report*, 79. See **Genoa.**) The trail had been a major Indian trail, which Daggett developed and maintained. (Freed, *Washo*, 79.)

Dr. Charles Daggett was one of the few doctors in the area. He performed an amputation of Sisson's frostbitten feet in 1856. (See **Thompson Peak.**)

"Mr. John A. ['Snowshoe'] Thompson . . . set out on his return journey at meridian on Wednesday of last week, taking his departure from the foot of Dagget's Cut-off, three miles above the Mormon station. The perilous passage of this almost precipitous pass was made in safety,

George H. Goddard, who surveyed a route to Lake Tahoe in 1855
and made the first drawing of the lake. (See the front cover.)

and our hero arrived at nightfall at Kelly & Roger's inn, situated on the
beach of Lake Bigler." (*Sacramento Daily Union*, February 4, 1856.)

Mr. W. W. Smith of the Alta Telegraph Office, Sacramento, "after
spending a couple of days in the [Carson] Valley, started back on the
5th at 2 o'clock p.m., on horseback. He came by the way of Daggett's
trail, and confirms our previous reports, that with the outlay of a comparatively small sum, the distance could be reduced at least ten miles,
and the road much improved. (*Sacramento Daily Union*, August 8, 1857.)

"In 1860 Kingsbury & McDonald surveyed and made a beginning on the celebrated graded road through Daggett's Pass, on the Eastern Summit." (*Sacramento Daily Union*, October 30, 1863. See **Kingsbury Grade**.) The Wheeler Survey listed "Daggett Pass" at 7,297 feet, and had the name on the map of 1881. (Wheeler, *Geographical*, 126.) A newspaper reported a post office "at Daggett's Run, to be called Daggett's Run P.O., Chas. D. Daggett, P.M." (*Sacramento Daily Union*, August 2, 1858.) However, this information does not appear in the postal archives. (Salley, 54.)

Daggett Creek was named "Haines Creek" on the *Markleeville* 30-minute map. Field investigators found that the stream is known locally as Daggett Creek, but the canyon through which the creek flows is Haines Canyon. (USGS. See **Haines Canyon**.)

Dardanelles Lake   California: El Dorado
Echo Lake

Browning in *Place Names of the Sierra Nevada* states that the namers of the Dardanelles features are not known. George H. Goddard's 1853 *Map of Sonora Pass* shows the name "Dardanells." (Browning, 52.)

The Dardanelles peaks may have been named in the 1860s by the men of the Whitney Survey because they saw a resemblance to the mountain castles that guarded the entrance to the Sea of Marmora (also spelled Marmara) in Turkey. This name was frequently used for mines and mining companies, perhaps because the Crimean War of 1854 made the name of the Dardanelles widely known. In a letter dated March 10, 1861, Whitney mentioned the Dardanelles Diggings in Placer County. (Gudde, 84.) In 1895 H. W. Turner wrote: "The [*Dardanelles* 30-minute] sheet is named from the very picturesque bluffs, composed of lavas, which bear the name of the Dardanelles, the highest point being known as the Dardanelle Cone." (Turner, 708.)

Deadman Point   Nevada: Douglas
Glenbrook

Origin unknown, but obviously the name suggests that this is a place where a man's corpse was found. It is possible that the name arose from the following incident.

"Fourteen persons have been drowned in Tahoe since its discovery by white men. The first was an unknown man in 1859. Three persons started from Glenbrook in a boat which they had built, intending to go to Sugar Pine Point. A wind caused the boat to capsize when close to land. Two of the men clung to the boat and were saved; the third tried to swim ashore and was Tahoe's first victim." (*Sacramento Daily Record-Union*, May 29, 1875.) The name appeared on the Wheeler map of 1878 as "Dead-man Pt."

Desolation Wilderness   California: El Dorado
Echo Lake
Emerald Bay
Homewood
Pyramid Peak
Rockbound Valley

Desolation Wilderness formerly was known as "Devil's Valley," "Devil's Basin," and "Desolation Valley." (Scott, 175, 480.) The name "Devils Basin" first appeared on the Wheeler map of 1881. In a letter to Robert Rice of the Inter-County Title Co., dated April 7, 1965, Ross Pierce wrote: "In the 'nineties I visited Glen Alpine a number of times and during two vacations about the turn of the century I worked as a guide or general roust-about there. . . . When I first heard of Desolation Valley, it was called Devil's Basin." (USGS.) The name was changed to "Desolation Valley" on the 1955 Forest Service map.

"It is its wild appearance that gives the valley its name, and not the feeling induced; for Desolation Valley is beautiful in its setting and most interesting in its contours. But no fish are in the endless chain of lakes, and only dwarfed trees grow in its rock-bound domains. Whenever the soil has collected in sheltered nooks, grass grows and flowers bloom. These tiny oases are very frequent and most charming in their surprises." (DeLaguna, 266.)

Preservation of this area began when the El Dorado National Forest was created in 1910. In April of 1931, 41,383 acres were set aside as the Desolation Valley Wild Area. In 1966 the US Forest Service proposed full wilderness status for the area, and an increase in its size to more than 63,000 acres. A bill enlarging, reclassifying, and renaming it "Desolation Wilderness" passed both houses of Congress in October 1969. (Strong, 161; Wood, 26–31.) The name "Desolation Wilderness" appeared on the 1969 *Pyramid Peak* quad. Desolation Wilderness, six to eight miles wide, fifteen miles long and 100 square miles in area, is one of the more heavily used wilderness areas in California. So as not to exceed the carrying capacity of the land, the Forest Service in 1971 began requiring permits for overnight camping. (Strong, 162.)

W. W. Price atop Dicks Peak. Photo by J. N. LeConte.

Dicks: Lake, Pass, Peak California: El Dorado
Rockbound Valley

"Dicks Pk." appeared on the *Pyramid Peak* 30-minute map of 1889. The peak was named for an eccentric Englishman, Captain Richard "Dick" Barter, also known as "the Hermit of Emerald Bay" or the "Hero of Robber's Roost." "Captain Dick Barter was an old sailor (or shell-back, as he expressed it), who was employed by Mr. [Ben] Holladay to remain on the place and keep things ship-shape." In 1870 he was sixty-five years old and had "lived in this lonely spot for about seven years. There is not a residence within miles of him, and often for weeks or months at a time, he does not see a human being. He is a

Robinson Crusoe in actual life." (*San Francisco Daily Alta California*, August 22, 1870.)

"In Ben Holladay's house at Emerald Bay is a masterly piece of workmanship in the shape of a full rigged man-of-war, with men, guns and all the usual appurtenances and appliances. This Dick made during his hermitage, and for the remainder of his time he floated idly upon the lake, took charge of Holladay's house and grounds, or worked upon his own grave! Strange as it may appear, on a rock island in Emerald Bay, he fashioned a grave out of the solid rock, built over it a house, erected above it a Catholic cross, and gave directions to have his body placed in the stony crypt. He loved the lake, and for hours at a time drifted about in his boat. At times he drank heavily, and when he felt the stupor of intoxication stealing over him he would row toward the middle of the lake, lie down in his boat and drift with the waves until he became sober. Poor Dick! he left Glenbrook one fearfully windy day much the worse for liquor, and off Rubicon Rocks his boat was seen to disappear. When the storm subsided his trusty boat was found crushed to minute fragments in the clefts of the rocks. One oar, much worn and chafed by rocks and waves, lay with the pieces of boat. The other oar was found three months afterwards in the same place, worn but slightly. The inference was plain. Captain Dick carried with him the last oar to the bottom of Tahoe. How it became detached from his death grip no one knows, but all his old friends regard this oar as a sad messenger sent to tell that Captain Dick's body has no further claims upon this upper world, not even upon the grave he prepared." (*Sacramento Daily Record-Union*, May 29, 1875. See **Emerald Bay** and **Glenbrook**.)

Mighels "discovered that one RICHARD BARTER was granted by the Examining Board for London, in the year 1848, a certificate as First Mate in the Mercantile Marine Service of the Kingdom. This said Richard Barter was the identical Cap'n Dick whose name is so closely woven in with the life, history and legendary lore of Emerald Bay." (Mighels, 252.)

Dollar: Creek, Point　California: Placer
Kings Beach

Washoe Indians called this point *diphEkhwO'tha*, meaning literally "white paint river." "The Washo obtained fish, porcupine berries, sunflower seeds, *cu'wE'thUkh*, and white clay with which they decorated themselves" (Freed, *Washo*, 81.)

On the 1863 Ives, Houghton & Kidder map, the point is called "Chinkapin Point."

Later it became known as "Observatory Point" when it seemed likely that philanthropist James Lick would build a large observatory there—but this did not happen. The observatory was built atop Mount Hamilton, east of San Jose, in the 1880s. (Wheeler, *Report*, 1291. See **Observatory Point**.)

In 1898 D. L. Bliss took title to the area when he formed the Lake Tahoe Railroad and Transportation Company. In 1916 Mrs. Lora Moore Knight acquired the land and built a cluster of chalets, which she called Wynchwood. (See **Vikingsholm**.) In 1927 San Francisco shipping magnate Robert S. Dollar, Sr. bought the property, including the sheltered cove. It was considered the "choicest residential site at Lake Tahoe." (Scott, 353.) The Dollar property was later subdivided.

The *Kings Beach* quad has the name "Observatory Point" on a triangulation station. "Dollar Point" was made the official name by a BGN decision in 1962.

Douglas County   Nevada
Glenbrook
South Lake Tahoe

The county was created on November 25, 1861. (Carlson, 100.) It was named for Stephen Arnold Douglas, (1813–1861), chairman of the US House and Senate Committees on Territories, vigorous advocate of westward expansion, and an ardent supporter of the Union. He is best known for the Lincoln-Douglas debates of 1858. (Lamar, 318–19.)

Duane Bliss Peak   Nevada: Douglas
Glenbrook

"Immediately behind Glenbrook rises *Dubliss Mountain* (8729') named after both the elder and younger Duane Bliss, father and son." (Rider, 276.) Duane Leroy Bliss, a Lake Tahoe lumberman, came out to California from Massachusetts via the Isthmus of Panama in 1850. He moved to Nevada in 1860 and became partner in a Gold Hill banking firm, which later merged with the Bank of California. Bliss acquired his first 160 acres of timberland in 1870, near Spooner Summit. (Scott, 491.) With Yerington he established the Carson and Tahoe Lumber and Fluming Company in the early 1870s. They held over 50,000 acres in the basin. (Strong, 25.) Bliss died December 23, 1907. (See **D. L. Bliss State Park, Glenbrook**, and **Spooner**.)

Duck Lake   California: El Dorado
Homewood

Origin unknown. "Duck Lake" appeared on the *Truckee* 30-minute map of 1940 and on the Forest Service map of 1944. (See **Buck Lake**.)

Eagle: Falls, Lake, Point   California: El Dorado
Emerald Bay

"Eagle Bay" was the earlier name for Emerald Bay. (Scott, 479.) Eagle Falls was sometimes known as "Emerald Bay Falls." (*Sierra Highlands*.) The name "Eagle Point" appeared on the Wheeler map of 1878. "Eagle Lake" appeared on the *Pyramid Peak* 30-minute map, 1889.

Eagle Creek, flowing from Eagle Lake, "plunges over the precipice and makes the foam-flecked Eagle Falls." (James, *Lake*, 133.) The creek name no longer appears on the quad map.

"Bald-headed and golden eagles are often seen in easy and circular flight above the highest peaks. In the fall and winter they pass over into the wild country near the almost inaccessible peaks above the American River and there raise their young. One year Mr. Price observed a pair of golden eagles which nested on Mt. Tallac." In September 1913 W. W. Price and George Wharton James were lunching on top of Pyramid Peak when an eagle bolted out of the clear sky. Its wings "made a noise as of a 'rushing mighty wind.'" (James, *Lake*, 303.) Washoe Indians believed that "Supernatural power can come from the deer, rattlesnake, water, 'water-baby' (a small, white, manlike creature that lives in streams, springs and lakes), bear and eagle." (Freed, *Aboriginal*, 42. See **Tallac**.)

Eagle Rock   California: Placer
Homewood

The origin of the name is not known, and there is no mention by Freed of the Washoes having been here. Although not the highest peak, eagles may once have nested here. "On the highest peaks eagles, prized for their magical feathers, nested." (Downs, 10.)

An earlier name for the rock was "Eagle Cliff." Photographer R. E. Wood made "Views of Lake Tahoe and Vicinity," including Idlewild. "Photographic negatives were made yesterday, by R. E. Wood, of Thomas McConnell's, at Idlewild, and also of Eagle Cliff. A large party of residents, may be seen sitting on the rocks." (*Tahoe Tattler*, September 2, 1881.)

Eagle Rock. "A large number of residents, may be seen sitting upon the rocks." Photo by R. E. Wood, about 1881.

East Peak; East Peak Lake   Nevada: Douglas
South Lake Tahoe

The name appeared on the 1944 Forest Service map. Carlson noted that "A number of orographic features are named for their relation to other peaks and ranges. . . . East Peak is southeast of Tahoe Village near the California boundary." (Carlson, 103.)

Echo: Lakes, Peak, Summit   California: El Dorado
South Lake Tahoe

"Away up above is Echo Lake, where there is a wonderful chorus of echoes." (*Sacramento Daily Union*, August 4, 1866.) "Echo Lake" and

"Echo Dam" were on the 1881 Wheeler map. The lakes have been used for sport fishing since the 1870s, and the not-so-distant meadowlands were grazed by livestock from the 1850s to the 1930s. In the 1850s John Kirk of Placerville began water development of Echo and Aloha lakes. In the spring thaw of 1911 the dam broke, and 2,000 acre feet of water deluged Lake Valley, washing Osgood's Toll House at the foot of Meyer's Grade from its foundation. In 1920 the Echo Lake dam was raised, and the two lakes were joined. (Scott, 175–77.) A post office was opened August 8, 1888. (Salley, 65.)

The route across Echo Summit was at first an Indian trail, then an emigrant road, and by 1863 was an improved wagon road carrying an enormous amount of traffic. (Brewer, *Up and Down*, 439–40.)

Scott lists the following former names for Echo Summit (Scott, 498):

Johnson Trail Summit or Hill (1848–1852)

Mickey Free Point (1852–1855)

Nevett's Pass or Summit (1857–1859)

Hawley's Summit (1859–1861)

Osgood's Summit (1861–1870)

Big Hill Summit (1861–1870)

"Johnsons Pass" first appeared on Goddard's earliest map (Goddard, *Sierra*), and on the von Leicht-Hoffmann map of 1874. It was also on the 1875 *Map of the Comstock Area*, the Wheeler map of 1881, and the *Map of the Carson Valley*, 1883. It is named for or perhaps by John Calhoun "Cockeye" Johnson, who explored Lake Valley in 1848. (Greuner, 9. See **Johnson Pass**.) Farquhar suggested that he found the pass in 1852, or perhaps earlier. (Farquhar, *Sierra*, 95.) Goddard wrote: "The Johnson Pass is the lowest of any of the central passes yet examined, and as such, most fitted for a winter road." (Goddard, *Report*, 118.)

"Mickey Free Point" was named for a bandit who, along with George Wilson, robbed and killed lonely miners, Chinese in their camps, and Ruddle and Howe (also referred to as the Stewart brothers) at Lake Valley in July of 1855. (*San Francisco Daily Alta California*, October 1, 1855.) "We continued down the fine level bottom of the valley, passing and leaving to our left the trading post, now deserted, where unsuspecting inmates were murdered in July last." (Goddard, *Report*, 112.) Free was tried on a charge of murder, found guilty, and hanged in Coloma on October 26, 1855.

"Some 5000 or 6000 people assembled before the appointed time. . . . Free had, according to his confession and the evidence adduced on his trial, led a long career of crime. He married a good, true and virtuous woman, whose precepts and example had he followed, would have deterred him from vice. He, however, robbed her of all her money, and left for California some years ago. Here he has been known as a thief, highway robber, and finally, it is satisfactorily demonstrated that he was engaged in several murders before justice overtook him. The crime for which he has just suffered the extreme penalty of the law, was committed some months ago. He was then in the region of Lake Valley, El Dorado, in company with one Kelly, Wilson, and others, where they encountered two traders. They decided to kill them. The particulars of the murder are thus given in the confession. . . ." (*San Francisco Daily Alta California*, October 28, 1855, reprinted from the *Placerville American*.)

In a letter to the California State Library dated November 6, 1980, James W. Gray wrote: "Mickie Free boarded with my grandparents (Mr. & Mrs. Young Gray) at the Lone Tree House which was located ½ mile below Mud Springs (now El Dorado). He borrowed Mr. Gray's gun & dog and used this gun to rob & kill some Chinese. He also killed the dog. He was hung for this crime." Mr. Gray enclosed a Bible left by Free and a song sung by Free on the gallows.

According to the *Daily Alta* article, Free said: "'I'll give you Miky Free's scaffold song.' Commenced, but after singing three lines, stopped, saying, 'Gentlemen, I can't go through with it, you must excuse me.'" Then Crane, who was also to be executed for murdering, sang "a hymn from manuscript, probably of his own composition, in which Free heartily joined." The words to the song donated by James W. Gray most likely related to Crane's hymn. Crane was known as "an enthusiastic spiritualist, and on this subject was regarded as a monomaniac." (*San Francisco Daily Alta California*, October 28, 1855.)

Mickey Free became something of a historical character; his murderous exploits were ever in the public mind. (Sioli, 153.) "We reached the summit of Johnson's Hill, at a little before 11 o'clock on Friday. Our first desire, of course, was to see Lake Bigler. . . . In the valley below us we saw the Hotel of Smith, and the cabin in which the Mickey Free tragedy was enacted, and which now does service as a stable." (*Sacramento Daily Union*, June 17, 1857.)

"The ride was further enlivened by Buoy's personal sketches of the owners of the different ranches—for the land is all claimed and mostly fenced—his details of the tragedy associated with the ruined cabin of the Stewart Brothers, who were murdered by Mickey Free and George Wilson—his stopping Indians of Captain Jim's dusky tribe, who hunt and fish at this season in the valley. . . ." ("A Cruise on a Mountain Sea," *Sacramento Daily Union*, July 30, 1866.)

Coincidentally, research uncovered another Mickey Free, half Apache and half Mexican, born in 1851. He enlisted in the Apache Scouts as a trilingual interpreter, and served with that organization until retirement. (A. K. Griffith. *Mickey Free, Manhunter.* Caldwell, Idaho: Caxton Printers, Ltd., 1969.)

The summit was the critical link in the road between California and Nevada. The name "Nevett's Pass" was for James H. Nevett, chairman of the Wagon Road Directors. (Scott, 362.)

"The grading of Nevett's summit is so far completed that the stage passed over the new road." (*Sacramento Daily Union*, October 5, 1857.)

"The new road *via* the Summit was opened a week ago, much to the satisfaction of numerous trains that have passed over it. It is not yet finished, and progresses slowly, the constant travel interfering with blasting out the projecting rocks, the only work now to be done. The road is of a very easy grade, substantially built, and will be finished ten feet wide, with fifteen turn-outs, and has been accomplished with great labor and probable loss to the contractor. I regret that funds could not be raised to make the road wider, for although perfectly safe, it does look ticklish to ride so near immense precipices as there are along it, particularly from the box of the stage on the off side going down, as I can testify to." (Ibid.)

"We left Placerville on Monday last, per Crandall's stage, for the purpose of examining the work upon the new road at the Summit. We found the road to that point very dusty and rough, owing to the great amount of travel upon it, meeting emigrant trains nearly the entire distance, driving with them immense bands of cattle. The most agreeable feature of the emigration is the large proportions of women and children; the latter in most astonishing numbers; their rosy cheeks and bright eyes shining out through the dust in merry glee, as we passed them." (Ibid. See **Pioneer Trail**.)

More than two years later, the final part of the grade west of Echo Summit still had not been completed. "The grade is not finished over this portion of the road, and its want is very sensibly felt, as it is, with one exception, the most difficult part of the journey. There are two steep and rocky ascents before reaching the summit, which is eight or nine miles from Berry's. . . . In the last of these level places a little stream takes its rise, whose waters flow eastward, and the traveler realizes now that he is passing out of the Pacific State, and is again connected, though it be only by the thread-like tenure of a rivulet, with those systems of rivers and lakes, the arteries of commerce, which feed the great countries belonging to the Atlantic. A hundred yards above the spring the road emerges from the forest and comes out upon a ledge of rocks, from which the eye takes in the magnificent view of Lake Valley. This is the Summit." (*Sacramento Daily Union*, November 15, 1859.)

The name "Osgood's Summit" was for Nemie Osgood. (See **Osgood Swamp**.)

The *Tahoe Tattler* on July 19, 1940 reported the "new Echo Summit Road open." Nineteen forty-seven saw the completion of a new all-weather road from Echo Summit to Lake Tahoe along the south shore. (Strong, 51.)

Edgewood Creek
Edgewood   Nevada: Douglas
South Lake Tahoe

A Washoe camp existed along this small stream, which enters Lake Tahoe at Edgewood. The Washoe name for the place is *lamwO'tha*. *Lam* means "mortar" and *wO'tha* means "river." The Indians collected berries, *cu'wE'thUkhO*; roots, *ma'sakha* and *sEsmE'*; and grass seeds, *matsilOlO*. (Freed, *Washo*, 78.) Martin K. "Friday" Burke and James Washington Small built a station here in the early 1860s. (See **Kingsbury Grade** and **Stateline**.) Edgewood was named by John Wales Averill, who in 1888 bought Small's 130 acres, and operated the Lake Valley Meat Market in conjunction with a dairy. Averill was also remembered for growing the largest rhubarb in the Tahoe region. (Scott, 237. See **Burke Creek**.)

El Dorado: Beach, County, National Forest   California
Emerald Bay
South Lake Tahoe

Charles Preuss, the cartographer on Frémont's first, second, and fourth expeditions to the West, had the legend "El Dorado or Gold Region" placed along the Rio de los Americanos and the upper course of the Rio de las Plumas on his 1848 map. "These must have been the very last details added to the map, for official information concerning the discovery of gold did not reach Washington until after Preuss's manuscript was placed in the hands of the lithographer . . . ." (Frémont, *Memoir*, from the introduction by Dale L. Morgan, xxxi.)

Nellie van de Grift Sanchez suggested that Spanish settlers found the land that was later called California so beautiful that they naturally made comparisons to the fabulous realm of El Dorado. She refers to El Dorado, a mythical king, as the "gilded one," described in the romantic tales of South American riches. Sanchez also referred to General Vallejo's story of adventurer and explorer Gonzalo Pizarro's (1502?–1548) companion, Francisco de Orellana, who wrote a fictitious account of an El Dorado, an opulent region of South America, where nature was filled with harmony and with wealth in the form of gold, precious stones, bountiful food, and springs. (Sanchez, 300–303. *Britannica*, v. 17, 146–47.)

El Dorado County was one of the original twenty-seven California counties created by an act of the state legislature that was signed by the governor on February 18, 1850. (Coy, 1–5, 97.) "El Dorado (the Golden) was applied by the early Spanish to a fabulous land of gold. The name was quite appropriately applied to that county in which gold was first discovered." (Coy, 5.)

President Taft established Eldorado National Forest by proclamation on July 28, 1910. It was formed by transferring forest lands from both the Tahoe and Stanislaus national forests. (Ayres, 1.)

Elbert Lake   California: El Dorado
Echo Lake
Origin unknown. In 1950 the DFG reported that the lake had formerly been called "Little Alberts Lake" or "Little Albert." The lake is about 2.5 miles south of Echo Summit.

Elk Point   California: El Dorado
South Lake Tahoe
Origin unknown. "Elk Point" appeared on the 1944 Forest Service map. The point is half a mile south of Zephyr Cove.

Ellis: Peak, Lake   California: Placer
Homewood
Jock Ellis, for whom the peak is named, had a dairy, then later a sheep ranch along the road from McKinney's to Georgetown. Ellis Peak is on the western ridge, about four miles due west of Tahoma. The name first appeared on the Wheeler map of 1881. (James, *Lake*, 159.)

Emerald Bay; Emerald Bay State Park   California: El Dorado
Emerald Bay
"Eight miles west of the Lake House, across the head of the lake, is Emerald Bay. This morning six of us went over to the bay in a fine, fast sailing 'jolly' boat, furnished by mine host, Van Wagner. We had a rip-roaring breeze, and the way we went along was a caution to snakes. We

reached the bay, and clambered up the side of the mountain to look at some charming little cascades. Then leaving the falls, with some apprehensions that we might know more about them before returning, we pushed on up the rough old mountain, anxious to reach a peak from which thirteen little crystal lakes may be seen. Climbing a steep mountain is the nearest thing to work that I know of, but persons in pursuit of pleasure do not easily tire. On and still on, up and still up. At length the top is gained. The view is far more grand than we had anticipated. We returned, feeling well paid for our toil. A strong wind soon carried us back to the Lake House. (*Sacramento Daily Union*, May 29, 1863.)

"There is a beautiful bay across the lake, at the base of the snow-clad peaks of the western Summit, called Emerald Bay, into which falls a sheet of water from a height of one hundred and fifty feet." (*San Francisco Daily Alta California*, July 1, 1865.) The name "Emerald Bay" first appeared on the Hoffmann topographical map of 1873 and on the von Leicht-Hoffmann map of 1874. In 1877 "Emerald Bay and I"(sland) were noted by the Wheeler Survey, and placed on the 1881 map. In 1877 Lt. M. M. Macomb wrote: "The bay is about two miles long by three-fourths of a mile broad, narrowing down at the entrance to a quarter of a mile. At its extremity is the summer residence of Mr. Ben Holladay, Jr., which is entirely concealed in a grove of aspen and willow. A more charming retirement it would be hard to find." (Wheeler, *Report*, 1281. See **Dicks**.)

"In the general freeze which has converted the lake into a sea of ice, Emerald Bay has been frozen solid. It is one vast ledge of ice from the surface of its transparent waters to the bottom. More than ever is that beautiful bay a gem of purest ray serene, crystallized as it is, and firm set within its own rock-bound shores. From some cause, best known to themselves, the fish, especially the trout, have fairly swarmed here. When the great and sudden freezing came, it imprisoned them by hundreds of tons all over the bay. There they are fixed, like a bee in a drop of amber." (*San Francisco Daily Alta California*, January 10, 1878.)

An article in the *Tahoe Tattler* of July 27, 1881 suggested that the bay "derives it name from a green color which its waters constantly wear." A post office was opened December 17, 1888. (Salley, 69.)

The bay was home to several grand residences, hotels, and campgrounds. Mrs. Knight's Vikingsholm still stands at the head of the beautiful, glacier-carved bay, but Holladay's Cottage, Mrs. L. N. Kirby's, Salter's, and Armstrong's Milflores no longer exist. (James, *Lake*, 224–25. See **Vikingsholm**.)

"EMERALD BAY is a beautiful land-locked harbor at the southwestern extremity of the lake, three miles long and a mile in width. The water is a beautiful emerald green, and is bordered by a narrow strip of forest, back of which jagged and rocky mountains rise in their rugged beauty to a hight [*sic*] of 5,000 feet above the lake level. At the western extremity, on a few acres of natural mountain lawn, shaded by cozy groves of alder, poplar and pines, Mrs. L. N. Kirby has located what is now popularly known as Emerald Bay Resort. Here is a small hotel, with large parlor and dining-room, surrounded by numerous nicely furnished little cottages. Boats and fishing tackle are free to guests, and these with swings, hammocks, croquet, and climbing furnish an abundance of out-of-door exercise." (*Sacramento Daily Union*, June 15, 1890.)

In 1913 Tahoe's Rim of the Lake road was completed. Mrs. Knight died in 1945. Harvey West purchased the land in 1949, and later donated half the value of the land to the state. The state paid West $150,000 for the balance. The Save-the-Redwoods League paid West $25,000 for the Vikingsholm furnishings. By 1954 the state had acquired a large portion of the private lands around Emerald Bay and contiguous to the D. L. Bliss State Park, creating the Emerald Bay State Park. In 1964 David C. Dunlap of the Sierra Club, Howard F. Fletcher of Friends of Emerald Bay State Park, and Save the West Shore of Lake Tahoe led the successful opposition to a west shore freeway and a bridge across Emerald Bay. (Strong, 87–89, 120. See **D. L. Bliss State Park** and **Camp Harvey West**.)

Fallen Leaf Lake   California: El Dorado
Emerald Bay

"Climbed Pyramid Peak. . . . Several pretty little lakes near the 'Fallen Leaf' lake, 1½–2 m. long, deep blue, towards summit of Pass." (Brewer, *Field Notes*, August 20, 1863.) Since this is the earliest mention of the name, Brewer may have been the namer.

The report that "There is a lake called Fallen Leaf Lake, in which a sheet of water falls" confuses the lake with **Cascade Lake**. The correspondent, who called himself "Stereoscope," visited only the east side of Lake Tahoe. (*San Francisco Daily Alta California*, July 1, 1865.) The name first appeared on the Hoffmann map of 1873 and on the von Leicht-Hoffmann map of 1874. Robert S. Wood suggests that the lake was named for a Delaware Indian chief—Falling Leaf—who served as guide for a Tahoe-Sierra exploring party in the late 1840s. (Wood, 218.)

Courtesy, Jim Hildinger

Fallen Leaf Lodge. Photo by Frasher.

Mark Twain remarked that the very pure and fine air "is the same the angels breathe." (James, *Lake*, 248.) In 1877 Wheeler surveyor Lt. M. M. Macomb wrote: "Fallen Leaf Lake (118 feet above Tahoe) is easily accessible from Yank's by a wagonroad which leaves the head of the lake [Fallen Leaf] at Gillmore's [*sic*] Ranch." Fellow surveyor Conkling wrote: "On the northeast shore of this lake are found pebbles of a great variety of rock, such as slate, basalt, granite, diorite." (Wheeler, *Report*, 1281, 1290. See **Gilmore Lake**.)

Fallen Leaf Lake became a popular resort area as early as 1906, when Mr. and Mrs. William Wightman Price moved Camp Agassiz, which had been situated in the canyon below Glen Alpine, down to Fallen Leaf Lake, and opened a resort and campground. Mr. Price, a Stanford graduate, was known as an educator and naturalist. Mrs.

Price, also a graduate of Stanford, took a keen interest in the Washoe Indians, who returned annually to the Lake Tahoe area, and from whom she collected Indian legends. One such tale related the origin of the Indian name for Fallen Leaf Lake, *Doolagoga.*

The tale was retold by Phil Townsend Hanna: "According to Indian legend, the lake was formed and named when a good Indian, harrassed by the Evil Spirit, tried to escape to the safe valleys of California. The Good Spirit gave the Indian a leafy branch. If the Evil Spirit approached, the Indian was to drop a bit of the branch, water would spring up and the Evil One could not cross it. The Indian started out, dropped almost the whole branch in terror when he saw the Evil One following him, and Tahoe was formed. Then later he had only a twig left with one leaf on it, and the Evil One still pursued him, so he dropped the leaf and Fallen Leaf Lake, Doolagoga, sprang into being and on its surface floated the little leaf, as many leaves now float in the fall of the year. The Indian escaped." (Hanna, 92.) There is some question about the origin of this legend; it has been suggested that its imagery is similar to that of Indians of the East Coast. Perhaps this is the source of the notion that "Fallen Leaf" is the name of a Delaware Indian.

The Fallen Leaf Lodge became a favorite place for educators and nature enthusiasts. Price helped develop nature study walks and nature games. He published a *Guide to the Lake Tahoe Region* in 1902, and a pamphlet entitled *Glen Alpine Lake Tahoe Forest Reserve California*, in 1906. Walter K. Fisher, who conducted the boys camp until 1917 when it closed on account of the war, wrote that Price "had the ability to infect others with his enthusiasm and love of nature." (Fisher, 50–57.) In a letter dated July 3, 1949 to Harriet Price Craven, owner and manager of Fallen Leaf Lodge, University of California Professor Loye Miller wrote that "Billy" Price erected "an altar to the spirit of the open air." (Miller, letter 2. See **Glen Alpine**.)

After W. W. Price died in 1922, Mrs. Price managed Fallen Leaf Lodge and maintained the emphasis on nature education. Miller referred to a summer school for public school teachers. (Miller, letter 1.) The *Tahoe Tattler* reported on the origins of the Nature Guide movement of 1926–1927, which was initiated by Mr. and Mrs. C. M. Goethe. The project began at the Tahoe Tavern as a cooperative effort between resorts, including Fallen Leaf Lodge, and educators who sought to awaken an interest in the natural history and biology of the Tahoe environment. (*Tahoe Tattler*, June 26, 1936.)

Stephen Mather, director of the National Park Service, arranged the transfer of the Nature Guide experiment to Yosemite. "The interest of John C. Merriman, John D. Rockefeller, and family was immediate and finally bore material fruit in improvement of Crater Lake Park and the whole Nature Guide Movement in America," including Glacier, Yellowstone, Rainier, and Rocky Mountain national parks. (Miller, letter 1.)

A post office was established at Fallen Leaf Lake on May 13, 1908, (Salley, 72.)

In 1911 eleven members of the Stanford faculty built summer cottages on higher ground above Fallen Leaf Lodge, an enclave now known as "Stanford Camp tract" or "Stanford Hill." (Scott, 145.) In 1912 or 1913 Mr. and Mrs. Carl Fluegge opened Cathedral Park resort on the western side of the lake, and catered to outdoorsmen. Fluegge was known as an expert climber, angler, huntsman, and guide. (James, *Lake*, 247–50.)

Fallen Leaf Lake Lodge was sold recently to Fallen Leaf Associates, which consists of twenty-five families who are renovating the structures and building new ones. (Craven, 12.)

Island in Emerald Bay.

Fannette Island. Photo by R. J. Waters.

Fannette Island   California: El Dorado
Emerald Bay

Fannette is most likely a corruption of the name Coquette. "That pretty fall has no name. There is a good deal of christening to be done about here. The island is called Coquette Island, for the reason inclosed in a champagne bottle which is placed in a crevice at the end. A party of Sacramento ladies and gentlemen visited this place some time ago, and one of the ladies named the island the Coquette, because, 'being the center of a brilliant circle of admirers attracted by her beauty, she still has a stony heart.'" ("A Cruise on a Mountain Sea," *Sacramento Daily Union*, August 4, 1866.) The island was inhabited by Captain Dick Barter, who worked as a caretaker for Ben Holladay, the founder of the Overland Stage system. (James, *Lake*, 224. See **Dicks**.)

Fir Crags   California: Placer
Tahoe City

These promontories above the northeast side of the Truckee River serve as the Tahoe City ski-jump hill. (Scott, 467.)

First Creek   Nevada: Washoe
Mt. Rose

First, Second, and Third creeks empty into Crystal Bay. The namer is not known, but obviously the names were given to the first three creeks one crosses when going from Stateline Point to Incline. (See **Crystal Bay, Incline, Second Creek, Stateline Point,** and **Third Creek**.)

Flagpole Peak   California: El Dorado
Echo Lake

Origin unknown, but doubtless it was named because there was once a flagpole on it. The summit is easily visible from the south side of Lower Echo Lake. The name first appeared on a Forest Service map in 1945.

Flick Point   California: Placer
Kings Beach

Named for three eccentric pioneer brothers—William, Joseph, and Nicholas Flick—from Ottawa, Illinois, all born on Christmas Day, in 1841, 1847, and 1851 respectively. Joe joined a New York circus and Nick worked in the mercantile business, until they all heard the call of the West. "Yessir, we settled right here on Carnelian Bay, and outside of falling off wagons, we haven't had a sick day since. . . . And as for fishing . . . say, I used to row from Flick's Point, (named for us) across the bay over by Brockway, and these big lake trout were so darned thick we could hardly swing an oar." (Interview with Joseph and Nicholas Flick in the 1920s, *Tahoe Tattler*, July 5, 1935.)

Floating Island Lake   California: El Dorado
Emerald Bay

"This lake covers an area of about five acres. Floating on its surface is a lawn-covered natural island, some twenty feet in diameter, which floats with such buoyancy as to carry a fishing party of from four to six people, who paddle it about the lake." (*Sacramento Daily Union*, June 15, 1890.)

"Two miles from the hotel [Tallac House], . . . rests Floating Island Lake, so named from an unanchored island of matted roots, grasses and shrubs, that floats upon its surface, and at one time also upheld a thrifty conifer." (*Sierra Highlands*.)

Courtesy, California Historical Society, San Francisco

Floating Island Lake, with its "thrifty conifer."

Folsom: Peak, Spring   Nevada: Douglas
South Lake Tahoe

Probably named for Tahoe lumberman Gilman Nathaniel Folsom, who along with Seneca Hunt Marlette owned property on the north shore, then sold it and in 1889 bought meadowland north of "Friday's" station from Burke's widow and renamed it "Hobart." The peak also was known as "Folsom's Knob." (Scott, 243, 247. See **Burke Creek**.)

Courtesy, Nevada Historical Society

Gilman Nathaniel Folsom, about 1870.

Fontanillis Lake   California: El Dorado
Rockbound Valley

Origin unknown. In a 1908 brochure advertising Glen Alpine the name is spelled "Fontinalis." The name first appeared on the Forest Service map of 1945. One might speculate that it derives from the Latin word *font*, from which we get the English words fount and fountain. Possibly the namer of this lake was showing his erudition by using a Latin word with an invented diminutive ending, and perhaps wanting the name to mean "a little spring." The lake is near the rim of Tahoe basin, three miles west by north from Mount Tallac. (See **Glen Alpine** and **Tallac**.)

Fountain Place   California: El Dorado
Freel Peak

Garret Washington Fountain and his wife Adeline came across the plains to California in 1849. He was recorded in the 1852 census as a miner, age 35. Later they established an inn called "Old Georgetown Junction House" at the crossroads of the Georgetown and Placerville routes. Their place provided shelter for immigrants and their livestock after the long mountain climb. (CSL.)

The Fountains built a log house and station near the headwaters of Trout Creek in 1860. (Scott, 379.) Their son David Broderick Fountain homesteaded 160 acres in sec. 25, T. 12 N., R. 18 E. on December 1, 1904—the location that now bears the name "Fountain Place."

Four Lakes   California: El Dorado
Caples Lake

The namer is unknown. There actually are six lakes—or four lakes and two ponds. The name first appeared on the *Silver Lake* 15-minute quad, 1956.

Freel Peak   California: El Dorado
Freel Peak

The name "Freel Peak" was first identified by Goddard as one among "Job's Group of Mountains." (Goddard, *South.*)

Boundary surveyors noted another name, "Bald Mountain." "Leaving the lake at its most southeasterly part, a trifle to the south and west of Lapham's Station, it [the boundary line] crosses the Kingsbury & McDonald road through Lake valley at a distance of about half a mile southerly from the station, and almost immediately commences the ascent of the high granite range dividing Lake and Carson valleys, being the eastern summit of the Sierras. The line crosses these mountains obliquely, crossing numerous deep ravines, perpendicular granite precipices and barren peaks, rendering progress very slow and difficult. It leaves Job's Peak and Bald Mountain, the highest peaks in the immediate vicinity within the State, emerges from the mountains into the valley of the West Carson about a quarter of a mile west of Carey's Mill. . . ." (*Sacramento Daily Union*, December 31, 1863. See **Kingsbury Grade**.)

"Job's Peaks" appeared on the Hoffmann map of 1873, the von Leicht-Hoffmann map of 1874, on the *Map of the Comstock* in 1875, and on the *Map of the Carson Valley*, 1883. In 1876 Lt. M. M. Macomb credited William Eimbeck of the US Coast and Geodetic Survey with naming the peak for squatter James Freel, a native of Illinois, a miner and rancher, who settled at the foot of the mountain. (Wheeler, *Report*, 1280–81; Gudde, 114; Maule, 6; *Great Register*.) "A small monument and a bottle containing records found on the summit showed that the peak had been visited September 15, 1874, by a reconnoitering triangulation party of the United States Coastal Survey." (Wheeler, *Report*, 1280–81.)

In 1876–77 "Job's Peak," "Job's Sister," and "Freel Peak" were noted by the Wheeler Survey and were on the 1881 map. "Freel's Peak" and "Freel's Pass" (summit of the trail from Lake Valley to Hope Valley) are listed in the Wheeler Survey *Report* of 1877. The name "Freel's Pass" has never appeared on maps.

The mountain was also known as Sand Mountain "on account of its two peaks being covered with sand." (Edwards, 92.)

Gardner Mountain   California: El Dorado
Emerald Bay

M. C. Gardner, for whom the mountain probably is named, built a railroad that ran down to the location of present Camp Richardson, and he also cut timber in the surrounding area.

"**The Resources of Tahoe.** We find them numerous and exceedingly interesting. Nearly a dozen hotels do a thriving summer business in attending to the wants of tourists, yet tourists bring only a small portion of the cash to Tahoe. The lumbering interests are immense. The high mountain walls which encircle the lake are covered luxuriantly with forests. The Carson and Tahoe Lumbering and Fluming Company are letting exceeding large contracts. M. C. Gardner alone has a contract to supply 60,000,000 feet of logs during the next six years. He supplies six million feet this year, and at the rate of 12,000,000 per annum thereafter. . . . Gardner is building a broad gauge railroad through Lake Valley to haul saw logs to the lake. The road when completed will be from four to nine miles, and will extend to the very shore. The heavy logs will be loaded on the cars in the woods, drawn by regular locomotive engines to the lake, and from thence will be towed by steamers in rafts to the Glenbrook mills. Maine lumbermen, with all their boasted laurels, must look to it lest California be the first to substitute railway cars for logging trucks, and engines for ox teams." (*Sacramento Daily Record-Union*, May 29, 1875. See **Glenbrook**.)

"Our busy fellow townsman, Mr. M. C. Gardner, is pushing his railroad. Even now it is in active use and operation, hauling logs to his breakwater by the lake's edge. Only a short mile from here is the breakwater. You hear the shrill whistle of the old 'Ormsby' locomotive as it invades these piney solitudes. (*Carson Daily Appeal*, August 14, 1875. See **Camp Richardson**.)

It was also suggested that Gardner Mountain was named for James Horace Gardner, the second white boy born in Carson City. He grew up at Tahoe during the logging boom, and died there at age seventy-eight. (*Tahoe Tattler*, July 7, 1939.)

General Creek   California: El Dorado
Homewood
Meeks Bay
Rockbound Valley

Named for General William Phipps. The creek also has been known as "Sugar Pine Creek." (BGN, *Sixth Report*, 320. See **Phipps**.) The Washoes fished at the mouth of the creek, which they called *dukhmE'EmwO'tha*, but never camped there for long. (Freed, *Washo*, 80.)

Genevieve, Lake   California: Placer
Rockbound Valley

The origin of the name is not known. "Lake Genevieve" appeared on the Forest Service map in 1945.

Genoa: Canyon, Peak   Nevada: Douglas
Glenbrook

Genoa, originally called "Mormon Station," was named by Elder Orson Hyde of Salt Lake City, who was the first probate judge in western Utah when Nevada was still part of the Utah Territory. "It is said that Elder Hyde renamed the place after the birthplace of Columbus because the cove in the 'mountain' reminded him of the Genoa harbor." (Carlson, 118–19.)

Early in September 1855 George H. Goddard reported: "Since I was here in 1853, a handsome grist mill has been erected, with a saw mill attached, which appears to do a thriving business. A court house has likewise been lately built, and several other improvements made." On September 21, Goddard wrote: "Rode to-day to the summit of Daggett's Pass with Merkley; when near the summit we met Dustin and Hancock returning from the valley. The Mormon party have been elected by a large majority. The Mormon Station has been chosen the County Seat, which is to be named Genoa, after the birthplace of Columbus." (Goddard, *Report*, 107, 114.)

"Genoa is the oldest and, until recently, has been the chief town in this section. It was settled by the Mormons, and by them named, probably. The discovery of a good reason or motive for the place being called after the supposed native city of Columbus might be almost as great a wonder as the discovery of America. It consists of thirty-two or three houses gathered near the 'Old Mormon Station'—a log house, still standing—fronts on one street, has two hotels, one store, one blacksmith shop, two groceries, two or three whisky dispensaries, and a billiard room. The town hugs the base of the eastern range of the Sierra Nevada, and is situated only a mile and a half north of the cañon through which 'the trail' (Daggett's) enters the valley." (*Sacramento Daily Union*, November 18, 1859.)

Gilmore Lake   California: El Dorado
Emerald Bay

Nathan Gillmore (apparently the correct spelling), 1830–1898, at thirty-six was listed as a farmer at Mud Springs, originating from Ohio. (*Great Register.*) In 1873 he brought cattle and angora sheep up to graze in the high meadows. (Sioli, 79.)

It is also asserted that owing to the illness of his daughter Evelyn, Mrs. John L. Ramsay, of Freewater, Oregon, the family traveled up to Tahoe on the orders of her doctor. "Accompanied by an old friend, Barton Richardson, of the James Barton Key family of Philadelphia, he came up to Tallac, with the ailing child and its mother. Being of active temperament he and Mr. Richardson scaled Mt. Tallac, and in returning were much entranced by Fallen Leaf Lake. Later Mr. Gilmore came to Fallen Leaf alone, wandering over its moraines and lingering by its shores to drink in its impressive and growingly overpowering beauty." (James, *Lake*, 233.)

The name "Gilmore" at Fallen Leaf Lake appeared on the 1881 Wheeler map. In 1889 Wheeler gave his name as "Gillmore." (Wheeler, *Geographical*, 318.) On April 10, 1886 Gilmore homesteaded 166 acres in secs. 13 and 14, T. 12 N., R. 17 E.; this is on the southeast side of Fallen Leaf Lake. On May 21, 1896 his daughter Evelyn patented 160 acres in section 22 of the township—land around Glen Alpine. "Gilmore Lake" first appeared on the *Pyramid Peak* 30-minute map, 1889.

Gilmore "is in all respects the pioneer of this region, and tourists owe much to him and his enterprise." (Mighels, 243.) Strong suggests that Nathan Gilmore may have been the originator of a proposal to make Tahoe lands "unavailable for private acquisition under federal land laws" and to protect the "beautiful thirty-six-square-mile block of timbered land [that] included Fallen Leaf Lake and many smaller alpine lakes that stretched into the heavily glaciated Desolation Valley.

"Gilmore expressed willingness to give up his own land claims if the president of the United States would incorporate Glen Alpine and environs into a forest reservation."

Warren Olney, vice president and a charter member of the Sierra Club, addressing the commissioner of the General Land Office, wrote: "Everybody is interested in preserving the property for the use of the public on the one side, against a private speculator [Baldwin] on the other."

"Enclosed with Olney's letter was a petition from president David Starr Jordan [of Stanford University], and forty-nine professors requesting protection for the township surrounding Glen Alpine. A second petition, with the signatures of President Martin Kellogg and nearly 150 professors, students, and alumni of the University of California at Berkeley, followed early the next month. . . .

"On April 13, 1899, one year after the death of the elderly Nathan Gilmore, President William McKinley signed the proclamation setting aside 136,335 acres in the southwestern part of the basin as the Lake Tahoe Forest Reserve." (Strong, 62–66. See **Angora Lakes, Baldwin Beach, Desolation Wilderness, Fallen Leaf Lake, Glen Alpine, Susie Lake,** and **Tallac.**)

Ginny Lake   Nevada: Washoe
Mt. Rose

Nothing has turned up about the origin of the name, but surely it is an adaptation of the name Virginia.

Glen Alpine: Creek, Falls, Spring   California: El Dorado
Emerald Bay

Nathan Gilmore is credited with the discovery of the mineral springs near Fallen Leaf Lake, where he first herded stock in summer and then later opened a resort. "Rambling through the woods, some two miles above the lake he came to a willow-surrounded swampy place, where the logs and fallen trees were clearly worn by the footprints of many generations of wild animals. Prompted by curiosity he followed the hidden trail, saw where a small stream of mineral-stained water was flowing, observed the deer, etc., had licked the stones, and finally came to the source in what he afterwards called Glen Alpine Springs." (James, *Lake*, 233. See **Gilmore Lake.**)

Gilmore's wife, Amanda Gray Gilmore, chose the name Glen Alpine from Sir Walter Scott's romantic poem *Lady of the Lake*. (James, 233.)

Roderick Dhu
'Twice have I sought Clan-Alpine's glen
In peace; but when I come agen

I come with banner, brand and bow,
As leader seeks his mortal foe.
For love-lorn swain, in lady's bower,
Ne'er panted for the appointed hour,
As I, until before me stand
This rebel Chieftain and his band!'
(*Oxford*, 213.)

Gilmore built a wagon road at this own expense from Fallen Leaf Lake to the Springs, and developed a first class resort. In the words of John Muir: "The Glen Alpine Springs tourist resort seems to me one of the most delightful places in all the famous Tahoe region. From no other valley, as far as I know, may excursions be made in a single day to so many peaks, wild gardens, glacier lakes, glacier meadows, and Alpine groves, cascades, etc." (James, *Lake*, 232.)

Another frequent guest at Gilmore's was Professor Joseph LeConte. "On ascending the cañon [from Fallen Leaf Lake] the glaciation is very conspicuous, and becomes more and more beautiful at every step. From Soda [Alpine] Springs upward it is the most perfect I have ever seen. In some places the whole rocky bottom of the cañon, for many acres in extent, is smooth and polished and gently undulating, like the surface of a glassy but billowy sea. The glaciation is distinct also up the sides of the cañon 1,000 feet above its floor. There is no doubt, therefore, that a glacier once came down this cañon filling it 1,000 feet deep, scooped out Fallen Leaf Lake just where it struck the plain and changed its angle of slope, and pushed its snout four miles out on the level plain, nearly to the present shores of Lake Tahoe, dropping its debris on either side and thus forming a bed for itself. In its subsequent retreat it seems to have rested its snout some time at the lower end of Fallen Leaf Lake, and accumulated there an imperfect terminal moraine." (LeConte, *Glaciers*, 129.)

"Indeed such glacial experts as Joseph LeConte, John Muir, and David Starr Jordan have united in declaring that the region around Glen Alpine gives a better opportunity for the study of comparatively recent glacial phenomena than any other known area." (James, *Lake*, 209.)

Surveying in the 1876 season, Alfred R. Conkling recorded: "A wagon-road runs from Rowland's along the eastern side of Fallen Leaf Lake to Soda Springs, two miles from Gilmore's ranch, on the lake. According to the aneroid, the springs are 325 feet above it. The temperature of the water is $46\frac{1}{2}°$ F. The spring-water contains carbonic acid, sesquioxide of iron, and sulphurated hydrogen. It is bottled and sold at Rowland's and other hotels on Lake Tahoe." (Wheeler, *Report*, 1293.) In the 1880s Gilmore sold the soda springs water—bottled, boxed, and labeled as "Clan Alpine Mineral Water." (Edwards, 92.)

"Nature seems to have spent her energy in perfecting this place [Tahoe] for recreation and health, for in addition to all that has been mentioned is an exact counterpart of the famous Buffalo Lithia mineral spring, so celebrated for its medicinal properties. The water carries in solution iron, soda, salt, and lithia, and the rejuvenating influence these waters effect can be demonstrated by experiment better than by description. Altogether this in one of the most popular places in the mountains, and some half a hundred guests (always including a goodly number of good-looking school-ma'ams), find hospitality extended at the rate of $14 per week. This includes unlimited opportunities for flirting, lots of pie, and the use of a brand new piano." (*Sacramento Daily Union*, June 15, 1890.)

Glen Alpine Falls was known earlier as "Modjeska Falls." Gilmore named the falls for Helena Modjeska, an actress of Polish origin, who while appearing in Virginia City traveled to Lake Tahoe, and expressed great enthusiasm for the beauty of Glen Alpine. The name "Modjeska Falls" appeared in *Glen Alpine Lake Tahoe Forest Reserve California*, a brochure published in 1906, and in *Lake of the Sky* by George Wharton James, but the name did not appear on a USGS map. (James, *Lake*, 232.)

In 1898 William Wightman Price established Camp Agassiz for boys at Glen Alpine. In a camp brochure he proclaimed: "To enjoy the mountains and all that is in them, to protect the forests and the game, to explore and make accessible for others the wild places, is the aim of Camp Agassiz." The camp was named for Swiss-born Louis Agassiz, naturalist, geologist, and teacher, and a professor of zoology at Harvard University. His method of teaching, which was "to give contact rather than information," completely revolutionized natural history instruction in the United States. "If you study nature in books, when you go out-of-doors you cannot find her;" and "It's not text-books we want, but students. The book of nature is always open." (*Britannica*, v. 1, 319–21.)

Some years later Camp Agassiz was expanded to include adults. On June 6, 1900 Price married a fellow Stanford University graduate, Bertha de Laguna. In 1906 the Prices moved the operation to Fallen Leaf Lake, where they ran Fallen Leaf Lodge. Mrs. Price continued to operate the lodge for some years after her husband's death in 1922. (Fisher, 50–57. See **Fallen Leaf Lake**.)

The social hall at the Glen Alpine resort,
designed by Bernard Maybeck. Photo by Frasher.

Price wrote several articles on Tahoe natural history: "Discovery of
a New Grove of Sequoia Gigantea," in *Zoe*, 1892; "Notes on a Collection of Mammals from the Sierra Nevada Mountains," in *Zoe*, 1894;
"Description of a New Pine Grosbeak from California," in *The Auk*,
1897; "Birds of the Placerville - Lake Tahoe Stage Road," in *Condor*,
1901; "Some Winter Birds of the High Sierras," in *Condor*, 1904. Price is
credited with the "discovery of the most northern stand of giant sequoia, a small grove of six trees, found on one of the streams flowing
into the Middle Fork of the American River, heretofore unknown to

naturalists." In addition, five species (two fish, a rattlesnake, a chipmunk, and a pocket mouse) were named for Price, who was an ardent traveler and naturalist his whole life. (Fisher, 50–57.)

The Glen Alpine post office, which was opened June 23, 1904, moved to Tallac in 1918. It was reestablished in 1929 and then transferred to Camp Richardson in 1947. (Salley, 85.)

Still standing near the soda springs is the social hall of the Glen Alpine resort, a large one-room structure of steel, redwood, stone, and glass, designed by the famous San Francisco architect Bernard Maybeck. Much of the Glen Alpine area is owned by the Lake Tahoe Basin Management Unit of the US Forest Service. (See **Gilmore Lake**.)

Glenbrook: Bay, Creek   Nevada: Douglas
Glenbrook

"This was the main camping ground for the Washo from around Genoa." They found both fish and berries near here; the location was called *daumaladuphwO'tha*. (Freed, *Washo*, 82.)

Captain Augustus W. Pray, native of Vermont, arrived in California in 1853, commanded a ship serving the Pacific Northwest, and moved to Lake Tahoe in the late 1850s. He and his three fellow land squatters, Murdock, Warren, and Walton, are given credit for naming Glen Brook, for the meadow with a brook running through it. (Scott, 265, 490.)

"The 'Glenbrook House' is situated directly on the main road to Carson City, at the base of the Eastern slope of the Sierras, and a few hundred rods distant from the shore of the lake. . . .

"The 'Glenbrook House,' as it first breaks upon the vision of the tourist, causes no little surprise; for he little anticipates seeing in these fastnesses of the mountains so large and really tasteful a structure. His astonishment is increased on inspecting the commodious apartments and the many creature comforts provided by the thoughtful proprietor. The hotel was built by Messrs. Winters and Colbraith. It has, within a short time, been materially enlarged, until now it has accommodations for one hundred or more guests. The total cost of the establishment cannot be less than $25,000. (*San Francisco Daily Alta California*, September 16, 1864.)

"Glen Brook" appeared on Hoffmann's map of 1873 and on the 1875 *Map of the Comstock Area*. "Glenbrook" is the name used on the 1874 von Leicht-Hoffmann map. In 1876 Lt. M. M. Macomb of the Wheeler Survey wrote: "Glenbrook is very prettily situated on a small bay. . . . A brook flowing through a deep and shady glen empties into this bay and gives the place its name." (Wheeler, *Report*, 1279.) In the same year

Alfred R. Conkling wrote: "Glenbrook, the most important settlement on Lake Tahoe, and the headquarters of the lumber trade, lies in a small bay. There is considerable arable land in this vicinity. A strip of productive land extends back from the lake for a distance of 2 miles, where it is called Spooner's Meadow. . . . A good wagon-road follows the eastern border of this sheet of water from Glenbrook to Lake Valley." (Wheeler, *Report*, 1289.)

Courtesy, California State Library

Sawmills in operation at Glenbrook.

In the 1870s Glenbrook had some 400 inhabitants, who were primarily engaged in the lumber industry with four sawmills in operation. In March 1870 Sharon, Bonner, and Ralston of the Bank of California organized the Glenbrook Hotel Co. It was not until 1873 that Yerington and Bliss came to Glenbrook and revolutionized the lumber industry. In 1875 a narrow-gauge railroad was built. (See **D. L. Bliss State Park, Duane Bliss Peak,** and **Ralston, Mount.**)

"There are three sawmills now running, and by the first of June two more will start. The Carson and Tahoe Company are building a magnificent first class mill at Glenbrook, and Spooner and Patten are erecting a good sawmill two miles southeast of Glenbrook, and have a contract for cutting 20,000,000 feet of lumber. To Mr. Rigby, of Glenbrook, I am indebted for the following estimates of the daily capacity of the mills and the amount they are to saw during 1875. The new mill at Glenbrook is called a double mill. One side squares the logs in readiness for the saws of the other side to convert it into lumber: Carson Company's old mill, daily capacity, 50,000 feet; amount to cut in 1875, 6,000,000 feet; Carson Company's new mill, daily capacity, 75,000 feet; amount to cut in 1875, 11,000,000 feet; Captain Bragg's mill, daily capacity, 40,000 feet; amount to cut in 1875, 4,000,000 feet; Glenbrook (F. Davis) mill, daily capacity, 50,000 feet; amount to cut in 1875, 6,000,000 feet; Spooner and Patten, amount to cut in 1875, 2,000,000 feet. Total to be cut in 1875, 29,000,000 feet." (*Sacramento Daily Record-Union*, May 29, 1875. See **Spooner**.)

"We had a great place at Glenbrook, over 100 head of horses; and the last Nevada Station of the Overland Stage trail. I can still remember well . . . Hank Monk (famed early day 'Knight-of-the-lash') rocketing the old Concords for Echo Summit on the way to Hangtown (Placerville) and California coast towns." (C. T. Bliss, interviewed in the *Tahoe Tattler*, June 28, 1935.) Both Dan De Quille and Mark Twain related the Horace Greeley trans-Sierra adventure with Hank Monk. (De Quille, *Bonanza*, 320; Twain, 121–22.)

"A friend of mine came down one evening with Monk from Glenbrook on Lake Tahoe to Carson City, fourteen miles, in forty-five minutes. The friend asked him if he ever rolled a stage over on that route, for the horses were at full gallop half the time. 'Oh, No' was the reply, 'when you strike a level grade ride your brake and let the stock go; but when you turn a curve, take off your brake and give the wheels full play, because to ride a brake around a curve when going lively might make you trouble.'. . . At last, after many years, Monk tipped a stage over. He never recovered from the humiliation of it, and died a few months later." (Goodwin, 225.)

Granite Lake   California: El Dorado
Emerald Bay

"Granite Lake" appeared on the Forest Service map of 1945. "Granite Lake is one mile from Bayview camp at the southeast corner of Emerald Bay. Glacial in origin, it nestles in a hollow at the base of Fleetfoot Peak. Seen only as a mirror for wind-swept pines yet its icy depths provide fine sport for the angler." (*Tahoe Tattler*, June 25, 1937. See **Emerald Bay** and **Maggies Peaks**.)

Grass Lake   California: El Dorado
Echo Lake

The outlet stream from Jabu Lake flows into Grass Lake, whose outlet is Glen Alpine Creek. (See **Jabu Lake** and **Glen Alpine**.)

Grass Lake; Grass Lake Creek   California: El Dorado
Echo Lake
Freel Peak

In 1855 Sherman Day crossed from Lake Valley over Luther Pass into Hope Valley, passing Grass Lake—which at that time had no name. "For about a mile the upper portion of the valley through which the pass opens, is occupied by a lagoon and marshy flat." (Goddard, *Report*, 80. See **Luther Pass**.)

George H. Goddard also described the area: "We crossed the marshy flat to the foot of the [Luther] Pass through which several small, sluggish streams flow; there is no direct water course or ravine from the pass, although the ground is springy over much of the ascent." A week later, on September 13, 1855, he wrote, "We crossed the flat of Hope Valley and camped at the foot of Luther's Pass, at a small spring." (Goddard, *Report*, 109.)

"At the top of the pass a swampy valley sloping to the opposite side affords a clear road, and we drive along the margin of a pond nearly filled with rank grass, and called Grass lake from this circumstance. The remainder of the road is good to Hope valley." (*Sacramento Daily Union*, November 15, 1859.)

"Over hill 500–600 ft. above Hope Valley, in granite. At summit, 'Grass Lake', with swamps - with gravel ridges across the valley at both ends of lake - probably moraines - there are very steep hills in canon to Lake Valley." (Brewer, *Field Notes*, August 19, 1863.)

Today the lake is referred to as a hanging bog, suggesting its transition from lake to meadow. "Marlette Lake" may be an earlier name for this quasi lake. Grass Lake Creek, which flows into the Upper Truckee River near Luther Pass, is also shown on the *Echo Lake* quad. The name "Grass Lake" appeared on the Wheeler map of 1881.

Griff Creek   California: Placer
Kings Beach
Martis Peak

The Washoes used the location where the creek empties into the lake "only as a resting spot and not as a full-fledged camping site." It was called *gumlE'phEl wO'tha*. (Freed, *Washo*, 82.) The name "Griff" may relate to Griffin's mill. "Not far from here [Agate Bay] a small creek enters the lake, about the mouth of which is some pretty meadowland. Griffin's saw mill is on this stream." (Angel, *Placer*, 404.)

The name "Griff Creek" appeared on the *Truckee* 30-minute map of 1940.

Grouse Lakes   California: El Dorado
Rockbound Valley

Origin unknown. The name refers to a bird nearly as large as a big hen that lives year-round in the conifer forests, where its main food, needle tips of pines and firs, is always available. Its summer diet includes several kinds of berries. Goshawks and martens are its chief enemies. (Storer, 263.)

Haines Canyon   Nevada: Douglas
South Lake Tahoe

J. W. Haines was born in Stanstead, Lower Canada, in 1826. He came to California as captain of the "Ohio train," arriving at Placerville on July 31, 1849. In 1859 he went to Nevada and settled in Douglas County. Haines attended Nevada's first Constitutional Convention. (Angel, *Nevada*, 383.)

On December 18, 1864 Haines secured a Nevada State franchise to operate a toll road, which started "from the foot of Kingsbury grade, thence four miles east to Esmeralda Toll Road, then northeast to Como." (Maule, 21.) Daggett Creek, in Haines Canyon, was known earlier as Haines Creek. "Haines Canyon" first appeared on the *Dardanelles* 30-minute map of 1898. (See **Daggett Creek** and **Kingsbury Grade**.)

Half Moon Lake   California: El Dorado
Rockbound Valley

The lake was named for its shape, possibly by the USGS. The name appeared on the first *Pyramid Peak* 30-minute map, 1889.

Hawley Grade Trail   California: El Dorado
Echo Lake

Asa Hershel Hawley, a native of Windsor County, Vermont, traveled the Overland Trail in 1852 at the age of thirty-nine. In his memoirs, written in 1883, Hawley recalled passing through Carson Valley before there were white inhabitants. In 1854 he operated a public house outside Placerville. (Hawley, 1.) "A bright moonlight evening's ride of seven miles, brought us to Hawley's, where we made our first Camp. . . . The total rise from Placerville to Hawley's is upwards of 900 feet, and one-half of this is made in the first ascent to the ridge. After which, the ascent is very gradual, and could be made much more so if required." (Goddard, *Report*, 96–97.)

After the State of California appropriated funds to build a road from Sacramento to Carson City, Hawley was the second pioneer to settle in Lake Valley, and in 1855 he opened the second trading post there. Martin Smith, a Pennsylvanian, was the first squatter; he established a trading post in 1851. According to Hawley, Smith did not spend the winter season in the valley. "Smith" appeared on the Goddard map, *Sierra Region South of Lake Tahoe*, and on the von Leicht-Hoffmann map, 1874. "Hawley's" appeared on Gibbes' map, 1866.

Hawley built a cutoff road that angled southward from Johnson Hill along the Sierra crest to present Highway 50, crossing at Echo Summit. From that point it dipped in a southerly direction to the Upper Truckee River, where it intercepted the Luther Pass Road about two and a half miles south of Meyers. According to the US Forest Service *Trails* map, "It was considered to be the first and only reasonable grade into Lake Valley." A more direct route replaced it in 1861. Sherman Day referred to "Johnson Hill" and to an unnamed shortcut that was Hawley's Grade. "But there is a lower point about a mile south of the present road, where it is supposed the summit may be reached by an ascent some two hundred feet less." (Goddard, *Report*, 81.)

An early traveler described the trans-Sierra journey: "Call this a rough road? This is a Nicolson pavement. There's a pretty rough road ahead; after we pass the summit. But it's nothing when you get used to it. Everything goes. We are going over Johnson's Pass and down the Hawley Grade." (*Sacramento Daily Union*, July 28, 1866.) Samuel Nicolson (1791–1868), a native of Plymouth, Massachusetts, invented a form of wood-block paving that was used in several cities. (*Sacramento Bee*, February 7, 1868.)

Together with James Green and Snowshoe Thompson, Hawley went around the Lake in his small boat. "[We] found the outlet but at that time we did not know its name but since then it has become known as the Truckee River. I was therefore one of the first men who ever navigated Lake Tahoe and one with Green and Thompson who found the outlet." (Hawley, 3–4. See **Thompson Peak**.) On August 20, 1878 Hawley patented 160 acres in sec. 17, T. 11 N., R. 18 E., near the foot of the road named for him. He died in 1899 in Yerington, Nevada at age eighty-six.

Haypress Meadow California: El Dorado
Echo Lake

James suggested that the name originated from hay-baling in this meadow. Hay was cut and baled, and then sold for $90 to $100 per ton in Virginia City. (James, *Lake*, 138.) "Today an old hay press remains to testify to the rugged pioneers who came to cut the lush meadow grass [from the valley above the Echo Lakes], bale it and then bring it by scow to Lower Echo and then to Placerville by ox cart." (*Tahoe Tattler*, August 3, 1937.)

Heather Lake   California: El Dorado
Pyramid Peak
Rockbound Valley

The *Pyramid Peak* 30-minute map of 1889 showed "Heather Lake." F. DeLaguna described the area: "Heather Lake has a wild, almost sinister, beauty. Its water is black, and its perpendicular rocky sides suggest a tiny gem in a deep setting. It is so far up in the mountains that the snows often lie on its banks all through the summer. On that July day we crossed many a little snow-field. It is named from the gardens of white and purple heather which border the south end of the lake. This is a low-growing plant, quite unlike the Scottish plant; yet the mountain lake with its small tiny island suggested, even in its sterner features, the scenery of the 'Lady of the Lake.'" (DeLaguna, 264–65.)

Heavenly Valley; Heavenly Valley Creek   California: El Dorado
South Lake Tahoe

During the earliest road-building period, beginning in 1859, the area's first sawmill may have been located on Heavenly Valley Creek. (Scott, 484.) The creek was known earlier as "Miller Creek." John G. Miller, a young Pennsylvanian, built the "Miller House" beside the creek on Pioneer Trail in 1862, and ran a dairy. By 1870 his butter was hauled by wagon to Carson Valley. (Scott, 382–83.) In 1955, oldtimers still recalled the earlier name. (USGS.) Since the Second World War, private developers have leased Forest Service land and built one of the largest and most popular ski areas in the Sierra. (Strong, 158.) The name "Heavenly Valley" is an obvious commercial creation.

Hell Hole   California: El Dorado
Freel Peak

The origin is unknown, but one might speculate that a cattleman found this half-mile stretch of swampy ground a hellish place to graze his stock.

Hidden Lake   California: El Dorado
Rockbound Valley

The name first appeared on the Forest Service map of 1945. The lake is just south of a chain of lakes, and although its waters flow into one of the lakes, it is not on the main stream that connects the chain—and thus was at first hidden from view.

High Meadows   California: El Dorado
South Lake Tahoe

An obvious descriptive name for a broad meadow at an altitude of 7,800 feet. Cold Creek flows through it. Earlier the name was singular—"High Meadow." (See **Cold Creek**.)

Homewood; Homewood Canyon   California: Placer
Homewood

Homewood was settled in the 1880s and 1890s. The post office opened on July 31, 1909. "A composite name for a vacation resort and marina on the west shore of Lake Tahoe." (Salley, 99.)

"A Homewood district was formed in 1889, 100 foot lots were laid out priced at $50.00 apiece, but they did not sell. Finally they were offered free of charge to any person who would build a substantial house." (Scott, 476. Scott's source was the *Tahoe Tattler*, 1936.) The Homewood resort hotel was built in 1913 and was managed by Mr. and Mrs. A. W. Jost. "The first place for the steamer after leaving the [Tahoe] Tavern. . . .

"It also boasts a unique feature in an open-air dancing platform, with old-fashioned music. It owns its power-boat for excursions on the Lake, and its fleet of row- and fishing-boats. A campfire is lighted nightly during the season, and song and story cheer the merry hours along." (James, *Lake*, 380–81.)

Idlewild   California: Placer
Homewood

The name suggests a timbered area, which it was when the Edwin B. Crocker family summered here on the north side of Blackwood Creek. They called their summer home Idlewild, from which the area took its name. "Idlewild. Leaving Tahoe City and passing to the right around the lake the first place that attracts attention is the beautiful private property of Mrs. Margaret E. Crocker, nestling among stalwart pines and occupied for the present season by the family and guests of J. B. Wright, of this city." (*Sacramento Daily Record-Union*, July 6, 1889.)

"Idlewild," the summer home of the Edwin B. Crocker family.

The von Leicht-Hoffmann map of 1874 showed the name "Mc-Connel" at this location. In 1880 Thomas McConnell broke up his lakefront holdings and sold lots to Yerington, Birdsall, Rideout, Lubeck, and Crocker. (Scott, 65.) F. Birdsall Esq. of Sacramento built the loveliest cottage at Lake Tahoe at an expense of three thousand dollars. He left Captain McGill, a very trustworthy man, in charge of the building. (*Tahoe Tattler*, September 2, 1881.)

Officially the location became "Tahoe Pines" with the establishment of a post office on March 21, 1912. (Salley, 218. See **Tahoe Pines**.)

Incline: Beach, Creek, Lake, Village   Nevada: Washoe

Marlette Lake

Mt. Rose

The Washoe Indians called the area *ma'goiyatwO'tha*. "The site is on the small creek just west of Incline. It was a favorite spot for the Indians from Washo Valley. Except for chokeberries, all Washo berries grew in the vicinity." (Freed, *Washo*, 82.)

The name evolved from the incline railroad in use here in the 1880s. W. S. Hobart and S. H. Marlette began a lumber business in Little Valley, east of the Sierra, in the 1870s. About 1878 they moved their sawmill to Crystal Bay, at the northeast corner of Lake Tahoe, where there was a plentiful supply of timber. However, the market for the lumber they would produce was still east of the Sierra—at Carson City and Virginia City.

With an infusion of money from San Francisco capitalists, Hobart and others formed the Sierra Nevada Wood and Lumber Company, and built what had the local name of the "Crystal Bay Railroad." The sawmill was on Mill Creek. A short distance from the mill was the foot of the incline railway that accounts for the proliferation of the "Incline" name. By 1880 the company had built a double-track, cable-powered railway 4,000 feet long. In that distance it climbed 1,400 feet, an average grade of thirty-five percent, with the maximum grade attaining sixty-six percent. From the top of the incline the lumber was sent to Lakeview in a flume—part of it of a most imaginative sort.

Courtesy, Nevada Historical Society

The Incline sawmill and the famous incline railway.

There had been a major fire in Virginia City in 1875. Following that event the Virginia and Gold Hill Water Company bored a 4,000-foot long tunnel through the Carson Range to tap Marlette Lake. The tunnel was seven feet high, the water company and the timber company were on good terms, and thus a flume was built inside the tunnel just above the flowing water. The lumber had an uninterrupted run from the top of the incline to Lakeview in the valley below. (Myrick, 425–29. See **Hobart** and **Marlette**.)

The town of Incline Village was established on Incline Creek in 1882. It had a post office from 1884 to 1895. (Carlson, 141.) The last major logging season apparently was in 1894 (Myrick, 430), and soon the railway was dismantled and the town disappeared. (James, *Lake*, 204.) The name "Incline R. R." appeared on the 1875 *Map of the Comstock Area*.

Indian Rock   California: El Dorado
Echo Lake

The name "Indian Rock" appeared on the *Fallen Leaf* 15-minute quad of 1958. This rock pillar is on the southwest ridge of Angora Peak.

Jabu Lake   California: El Dorado
Echo Lake

The name is a composite of the first two letters of the first and last names of Jack Butler, who was a member of the Mt. Ralston Fish Planting Club. (Hildinger from Darrell Pierce, son of Ross Pierce.) Other similarly derived names in this vicinity are "Ropi" for Ross Pierce, "Waca" for Walter Campbell, "Gefo" for George Foss, and "Toem" for Tom Emery. (Hildinger letter, 1987; Tisher, 1965 letter to USGS.)

Jacks Peak   California: Placer
Rockbound Valley

The name appeared on the Wheeler map of 1881. Its uncertain origin is attributed to a Placerville miner and native of Missouri, Hardin Green Jacks, or to a man who settled in Jacks Valley, near Carson. (Scott, 465.)

Jakes Peak   California: El Dorado
Emerald Bay

The peak of 9,187 feet, located northwest of Emerald Bay above D. L. Bliss State Park, is named for Jeffrey "Jake" Smith (1954–1982), and in honor of other persons who also died in an avalanche in the Alpine Meadows Ski Area on March 31, 1982. (BGN, 1985.)

Jobs Sister   California: Alpine
Freel Peak

Moses Job, an early Mormon settler, ran a store located near the eastern base of Jobs Peak. Maule suggested that the adjacent peak is named in memory of his sister. (Maule, 6.) In 1855 George H. Goddard placed flags on "Job's Peak." (Goddard, *Report*, 104.) The name "Job's

Group of Mountains" appeared on a Goddard map. (Goddard, *South*.) The von Leicht-Hoffmann map of 1873 named the peaks "Jobs Peaks." The Wheeler Survey map of 1881 applied the names "Jobs Sister," "Jobs Peak," and "Freel Peak" to the group.

John A. Thompson, the "Expressman," reported to the *Placerville Democrat* on May 23, 1857: "Our late townsman, Moses Job, arrived from Carson Valley, where he now resides, yesterday about noon. He reports the grain crop as looking well. On his way down, he met quite a number of persons going over the mountains on trading expeditions, and others *en route* to the States. Mr. J. reports the grass as abundant in the valley, and the stock as looking very fine, a supply from whence to this region, may be looked for in the fall. The miners in Gold Cañon, he reports as still doing well." (*Sacramento Daily Union*, May 25, 1857. See **Freel Peak** and **Thompson Peak**.)

Johnson Pass   California: El Dorado
Echo Lake

Colonel Johnson, for whom or by whom this pass was named, was among the earliest Tahoe road builders.

"In conformity to your [Hon. S. H. Marlette, Surveyor General] instructions, I [George H. Goddard] have kept a full barometrical register for heights throughout the whole journey from Sacramento, through Placerville, by the old Carson Pass, and back again by the Johnson road to Placerville.

Height above Sea.

Placerville	1,755.2	feet
Old Carson Road—west Summit	9.036.1	"
" " " Red Lake Valley	7,175.9	"
" " " East summit or main Divide	7,972.9	"
Johnson Road, west summit or main Divide	6,743.4	"
" " Bigler Lake Valley	5,961.0	"
" " East or Daggett's Summit	6,824.6	"
Carson Valley, Mormon Station	4,337.0	"
" " Cary's Mill	5,032.5	"
Luther's Pass	7,175.0	"
Hope Valley (head of Carson's Canon)	6,488.7	"

"From the above it will be seen that the highest pass on the Johnson route is more than two thousand feet lower than that on the old Carson road. . . . When I crossed in the winter of 1853, the other road was utterly impassable, while the snow on the Johnson road, in its deepest place, did not exceed three or four feet, and for the greater part of the distance there was not more than six inches to a foot of snow. . . . By following the new pass, now called Luther's pass, from Bigler Lake Valley to Hope Valley, the descent is made easy, could the narrow valley between the Johnson pass, and Luther's pass be bridged over, by a lofty viaduct, of all the routes yet known, this would be the one for the Pacific Railroad, as there need be no grade upon it, exceeding 100 feet to the mile." (*San Francisco Daily Evening Bulletin*, October 8, 1855.)

"I [Sherman Day] notice that several writers and speakers allude to the road surveyed by me between Placerville and Carson Valley as the 'Johnson's Cut-Off' road, and having, as some of them say, formerly passed over Johnson's Cut-Off, they proceed to draw a comparison between the route and their own favorite route. I wish, through you, to protest against this, and to inform such persons that the route surveyed by me is not Johnson's Cut-Off at all.

"The two roads do not pass either the eastern or the western summit of the Sierra at the name in point. It is true that, for about nine or ten miles on this side of the western summit, at and near Slippery Ford [Twin Bridges], the two roads touch or approach each other somewhat as two crooked sticks laid side by side might do. At each end of the ten miles they diverge, and are not again coincident except for a short distance near Placerville, among the permanent settlements.

"I will state the points of difference between the two routes, to do which permit me to begin near the middle, on the western summit. My road crosses the western summit about one mile south of Johnson's, and accomplishes a descent of 1,000 feet into Lake Valley by a uniform grade of five degrees, extending for a distance of about two miles. [Day's road was roughly on the route of present U.S. 50 at Echo Summit.] Johnson's road makes an equal descent to the same valley in three quarters of a mile, with grades varying from ten to twenty-three degrees. I do not intend, by this comparison, to reflect on Col. Johnson's skill as a road maker. He did the best he could with the limited means at his disposal, and deserves much credit for having opened a road passable for wagons where before it was scarcely passable for mules.

"At the foot of the hill Johnson's route turns northeast, along the level plain of Lake Valley, to the southeast corner of Lake Bigler, a distance of about two miles. Here the road climbs several of the lofty spurs that make down from the eastern summit to the Lake, and descends also into the valleys between the spurs finally crossing the eastern summit by a very easy pass near Eagle ranch." (*Sacramento Daily Union*, May 19, 1857. See **Lake Valley**.)

Kalmia Lake   California: El Dorado
Emerald Bay
Rockbound Valley

The name refers to alpine laurel, *Kalmia polifoia*, an evergreen shrub, found along lake borders, in meadows, and swampy places up to timberline. Pale alpine laurel is deadly to sheep and cattle. (Storer, 138.)

The name appeared in the 1909 *Glen Alpine Lake Tahoe Forest Reserve, California* pamphlet. An earlier spelling, "Kalmeia," was changed to "Kalmia" to agree with the botanical name of the shrub. (USGS, October 19, 1956.) "Kalmia Lake" is found on the 1958 *Fallen Leaf* 15-minute quad. (See **Glen Alpine** and **Azure Lake.)**

Keiths Dome   California: El Dorado
Echo Lake

Named for pioneer W. F. Keith. (Scott, 466.)

Kings Beach (Community)   California: Placer
Kings Beach

The community is named in honor of Joe King, who is said to have obtained Robert Sherman's property west of Griff Creek in an all-night poker game in 1925. (Scott, 333. The "west" may be an error, since Kings Beach is east of Griff Creek.) King ran a speakeasy called Squirrel Inn, and made bootleg whiskey at his "goat ranch on the Truckee River." Aimee Semple McPherson held revival meetings in Moana Villa's dance hall across from King's Squirrel Inn in Homewood. (Scott, 45, 94. See **Griff Creek**.) Kings Beach developed into a flourishing town with motels, theaters, markets, stores, cafes, and homes. A post office was established March 25, 1937, but was closed on December 31, 1942. (Salley, 112.) In 1956 J. H. F. Fredricks of the USGS reported that they considered changing the quad name to *Squaw Valley* in recognition of the 1960 Winter Olympics, but decided against it.

Kingsbury Grade   Nevada: Douglas
South Lake Tahoe

"In 1860 Kingsbury & McDonald surveyed and made a beginning through Daggett's Pass, on the Eastern Summit, and opened it to the public in 1861. In the Fall of that year they began work on their grade into Lake Valley, which they completed in 1862, and at the same time opened a good road through the valley. We do not know the amount of capital invested, but it must have been largely over $50,000."

(*Sacramento Daily Union*, October 30, 1863. See **Daggett Pass**.) The name first appeared on the *Township Lines* map, surveyed by Lawson in 1861.

Kingsbury Grade served as a primary route for early trans-Sierra travel. One of the area's first stations was started in the early 1860s by Martin K. "Friday" Burke and James Washington Small at the Tahoe end of the road. The ride through Lake Valley "was to us one of unalloyed pleasure. At Friday's, twelve miles from the first summit, commences the ascent to the second, which is accomplished in about five miles. The road is a very good one, though rather steep in places, it being the continuation westward of the toll grade of McDonald & Kingsbury, down the eastern summit to Carson Valley. The ride up this ascent will give you frequent glimpses through the trees of the lake, which tempt one to stop and turn aside to see. . . . About half way up, a solitary German has his cabin by an excellent watering place, and there furnishes the inevitable 'lager,' with coffee and pies. . . . [We] came down the fine grade that has almost immortalized the name and genius of its designer, Kingsbury. I do not believe there is a finer specimen of engineering in this country than this grade." (*Sacramento Daily Union*, July 20, 1861. See **Edgewood**.)

"The proprietors of the 'Kingsbury Grade' say it has cost them $15,000—but I *guess* that is a—ahem! too much! But be it more or less, the rather steep tolls charged thereon will soon make the pockets of the stockholders whole." (*Sacramento Daily Union*, August 7, 1862.)

Tolls ranged from 37 and ½ cents at Clarksville to $2.50 at Kingsbury & McDonald, which was the highest toll. "The Kingsbury & McDonald grade, down the Eastern Summit into Carson Valley. Tolls $2.50; 25 cents each for extra animals; return teams half price." (*Sacramento Daily Union*, August 13, 1862.)

"Very near daylight, we arrived at the first summit of the Sierra, after which we sped along swiftly down its eastern slope, reaching the celebrated Kingsbury grade about sunrise. This is the most delightful portion of the ride, reminding one forcibly of a spiral staircase as we made the descent from steep to steep on the sides of the mountain. Down we went, and when we got to the last declivity, rushed furiously on into the valley below." (*Sacramento Daily Union*, June 22, 1863.)

Kiva Beach   California: El Dorado
Emerald Bay

Kivas were ceremonial chambers of the Anasazi Culture of the American Southwest. They were used by the men as places for meeting and for holding secret religious rites. "They were circular, subterranean structures which lay to the south or southeast of houses. Walls were of masonry, and there were encircling benches in which pilasters were often incorporated. Roofs were normally cribbed, and entrance was usually through the smoke-hole in the center . . . ." (Wormington, 64.)

One wonders at the origin of this name, or at the rationale for naming this beach "Kiva"—an Indian name, but unrelated to the Washoe. (See **Pope Beach**.)

Knee Ridge   California: Placer
Homewood

The name is on both the 1944 Forest Service map and the 1955 *Tahoe* 15-minute map. It most likely refers to the shape of the ridge as seen from Quail Lake. (See **Quail Lake**.)

Lake Forest   California: Placer
Kings Beach

Lake Forest Post Office was established April 16, 1947, and was closed on October 31, 1953. (Salley, 115. See **Antone Meadows** and **Burton Creek**.)

Lake Tahoe State Park   Nevada: Carson City, Douglas, Washoe
Glenbrook
Marlette Lake

In 1964 Nevada authorized a park of 13,500 acres with 7.5 miles of shoreline. Legal action was taken in order to acquire the Whittell property, and a jury decided in favor of the state park in November 1967. "Other lands were added, and the Lake Tahoe Nevada State Park soon encompassed more than 13,000 acres, including some of the most beautiful beaches and vistas of the lake." (Strong, 83, 89, 94.)

Lake Valley   California: El Dorado
Echo Lake
Emerald Bay

Two ethnographic sites were located in this area. One was along the Upper Truckee River about 200 yards east, and one and one quarter miles from Lake Tahoe. It was called *ImgiwO'tha,* meaning "river of the cutthroat trout," (*salmo henshawi*). The other site was called *mathOcahuwO'tha,* for "river of the white fish," (*Coregonus williamsoni*), which is the present Trout Creek. (Freed, *Washo*, 78.)

It is not known who coined the name "Lake Valley," but it was already in use in 1853, and it was being asserted that there was a "discovery of gold, of great purity, in Lake Valley, upon Johnson's route to Carson Valley." (*Placerville Herald*, September 24, 1853.) "Preparations are being made by Mr. Smith for a winter's residence at Lake Valley, though situated between the two highest summits of the Sierras. It is the Valley in which Lake Bigler is situated, and it is the intention of Mr. Smith to build a suitable boat, with which, in the spring, to explore the entire shores of this Lake, more than fifty miles in length, from north to south, and from three to ten wide, abounding in fishes of several varieties, and is the locality of one of the most remarkable caverns in the world. . . . Lake Valley, with its magnificent Lake, its immense crater of an extinct volcano, with its grottoes, and fields of wild strawberries ripening in August, will ere long become of world-wide renown as a place of summer resort." (*Placerville Herald*, October 8, 1853.) Most early visitors overestimated the size of Lake Tahoe, and incorrectly assumed it to be of volcanic origin. (See **LeConte, Lake.**)

In 1855 George H. Goddard wrote: "Sept. 2. Sunday.—Walked some two miles down the valley. There were a number of currant bushes near the trail, some of which were loaded down with remarkably fine currants, nearly as large as gooseberries and fine flavored. . . . Sept. 14.—Bigler Lake is a noble sheet of water, from fifteen to twenty miles in length by six to seven in width; we arrived at its shore at dusk, and camped at the point of timber which forms the eastern boundary of the swamps on the southern end of the lake. . . . A dense forest spreads out from this point (my station on the granite knob [probably Tahoe Mountain], not heard it spoken of under any name and believe it is unexplored) of our observations in every direction, except along the swampy flats before mentioned. The ground in many places is literally covered with strawberry vines, or sun-flowers. The whole bed of this valley is composed of granitic sand, and banks of pebbles, which in many cases appear sorted by the action of water." (Goddard, *Report*, 113–14.) "Lake Valley" appeared on a Goddard map. (Goddard, *South.*)

"Messrs. Gilbert & Garrish, who recently arrived from Salt Lake, with some 600 head of cattle, have driven them to Lake Valley to summer there. This is the valley in which Lake Bigler is situated, and is about eight miles west of Genoa, between two ridges of mountains." (*Sacramento Daily Union*, July 7, 1857.)

"In half an hour after leaving the summit the stage halts before the door by 'Smith's,' where a change of horses takes place. There are two public houses in Lake Valley, the one just mentioned and the other kept by the member of the Assembly elect from this district [Robert Garwood Dean, proprietor of the Sierra House]. The latter has been recently put up and offers more inviting entertainment than the old established inn." (*Sacramento Daily Union*, November 15, 1859.)

The first official post office opened at Lake Valley on September 17, 1861. (Salley, 116.) However, Martin Smith, Lake Valley's first settler, was reported to be the first postmaster. (*Sacramento Daily Union*, August 2, 1858.) Inasmuch as Smith's trading post was the first one in Lake Valley, perhaps it served for a while as an unofficial post office. The Wheeler map of 1881 showed "Lake Valley P.O."

In 1875 Professor Joseph LeConte described the former Lake Valley Glacier: "This great glacier flowed northward down Lake Valley, and, gathering tributaries from the summit ridges on either side of the valley, but especially from the higher western summit, it filled the basin of Lake Tahoe, forming a great *mer de glace,* 50 miles long, 15 miles wide and at least 2,000 feet deep and finally escaped northeastward to the plains." (LeConte, *Glaciers*, 126.)

The name Lake Valley remains in use, as in Lake Valley Branch Library, but the town that grew and filled in the valley is now called South Lake Tahoe. (See **South Lake Tahoe.**)

LeConte, Lake   California: El Dorado
Pyramid Peak

Named for Professor Joseph LeConte (1823–1901), professor of geology at the University of California at Berkeley, 1869–1901. LeConte was the author of two Tahoe-related publications: "Ancient Glaciers of the Sierra," *The American Journal of Science and Arts* 10, 1875 (Third Series); and "Ramblings Through the High Sierra," *Sierra Club Bulletin* 3, no. 1, January 1900. (The original edition of the journal was privately printed in 1875 as *A Journal of Ramblings, Through the High Sierra of California,* and was republished by the Sierra Club in 1960.)

Lily Lake   California: El Dorado
Echo Lake
Emerald Bay
Homewood

Wood suggested that Nathan Gilmore discovered this lake in 1863. (Wood, 24.) The 1909 pamphlet *Glen Alpine Lake Tahoe Forest Reserve, California* described Lily Lake. (Price, *Glen Alpine.*) "On a higher level lies Lily Lake, where fishermen, whose oars are 'lacquered in diamond' are paddling among great golden lily bowls upheld on broad salvers, green and garnet. Here are lilies with a tropic glory walled in by cold, gray granite bowlders." (Markham, 300. See **Gilmore** and **Glen Alpine**.)

Lincoln: Creek, Park   Nevada: Douglas
Glenbrook
  Lincoln Creek flows from Genoa Peak to Lake Tahoe. Its most obvious but unestablished reference is to President Abraham Lincoln. The Civil War and allegiance to the Union were issues among many pioneers. (See **Tahoe, Lake**.)

Little Round Top   California: El Dorado
Caples Lake
  A descriptive name for a smooth, round-topped mountain.

Logan: Shoals, House Creek
North Logan House Creek   Nevada: Douglas
Glenbrook
  Named for Robert Logan, who together with Wellington Stewart ran Logan House. In 1863 Logan acquired the property south of Glenbrook, with its beautiful views of the lake and surroundings, and by 1864 was doing a brisk business in the two-story hostelry—but all was lost to back taxes in 1866. E. R. Cox, acting for Henry Marvin Yerington, took possession of the land and improvements. In 1870 Yerington acknowledged ownership of the "ghost hotel." By the 1890s Logan House was gone. (Scott, 257–59.)
  On January 1, 1957 William M. Bliss wrote: "I greatly appreciate this [name change] being made and I am sure that Logan Shoals will be more familiar to the Tahoe residents than the former name of Glenbrook Rocks." (Bliss letter to USGS.)

Lonely Gulch   California: El Dorado
Homewood
Meeks Bay
  The word gulch is defined as "A narrow and deep ravine, with steep sides, marking the course of a torrent; especially one containing a deposit of gold." It may have derived from an earlier use meaning "A heavy fall." (*OED*, 1226.) The present use of the word, to refer to a depression, gully, or ravine, became the vogue during the California gold rush.

Lost Corner Mountain   California: Placer
Homewood

The origin is unknown, but it could be a name given by a surveyor —referring to an old corner marker of a section or township that a later surveyor could not find. The name appeared on the *Truckee* 30-minute map in 1940.

Lost Lake   California: El Dorado
Homewood

Near Lost Corner Mountain. The name appeared on the *Truckee* 30-minute map of 1940.

Lost Lake   California: El Dorado
Echo Lake

This tiny lake lies beneath Keiths Dome at the headwaters of Alpine Creek. Because it was so remote, it was "lost"—until it was found. The name appeared on the Forest Service 1945 quad and on the *Fallen Leaf* 15-minute quad, 1955. (See **Keiths Dome.**)

Lower Prey Meadows   Nevada: Carson City
Glenbrook

According to M. G. Larkins of the USGS, the names "Lower Prey Meadows," "China Gardens," and "Montreal Canyon" were submitted by the Forest Service. Although spelled differently, the name Prey certainly pertains to the earliest settler of the area, Captain Augustus W. Pray, who was possibly wrongly identified as N. W. Pray.

"As early as 1861, Mr. N. W. Pray purchased land in this charming valley, which, together with the timbered slopes of the adjacent hills, comprises a tract of one thousand acres. Although at an elevation of six thousand feet above the level of the sea, the soil of the valley is well adapted to the growth of vegetables, and for cereals cannot be excelled by the lowlands of the far distant Sacramento.

"As an evidence of the fecundity of the soil, it may be stated, that Mr. Pray last fall dug twenty-three pounds and seven ounces of potatoes from a small hill, and close by cut three tons of oats from one acre of ground. Barley and grasses flourish finely in this valley, despite the blasts which sweep down from the snow-clad peaks, two thousand feet above even this Alpine height. The stock raised here commands ready sales at good prices, in the Nevada markets, albeit the home consumption is considerable. Potatoes bring five cents per pound, and hay twenty dollars per ton.

"But the chief article of export from the Tahoe Valley is lumber, immense quantities of which are manufactured here and in the vicinity. On the borders of the Lake, immediately in the rear of the 'Glenbrook House,' Pray has erected a saw mill now driven by steam power, which cuts some twenty-four thousand feet of lumber *per diem*." (*San Francisco Daily Alta California*, September 16, 1864.)

Courtesy, Nevada Historical Society

Augustus W. Pray, at Carson City, 1863.

"A correspondent of the *Bulletin*, writing from Pray's Mills (N.T.) [Nevada Territory], has the following: This location is on the easterly side of Lake Tahoe (formerly 'Lake Bigler'), about equi-distant from the head of the Lake and Carson City. There is a fine water power here, and large quantities of excellent timber. As soon as the new road, which is now being rapidly pushed forward, is completed, this lumber will readily find its way to a good market." (*Sacramento Daily Union*, June 11, 1863.)

"Colbrath, a gentleman from Virginia City, having bought five acres of Captain Pray's place (Pray's Mill) at Lake Tahoe, is about putting up a fine hotel. . . . Wellington Stewart of Carson has one already nearly completed a mile further south." (*Sacramento Daily Union*, August 26, 1863.) The name "Pray's landing" was noted as a regular stop of the Lake Tahoe schooner in the same paper on December 9, 1863.

"Coming from Carson, we first strike the lake at the residence of Captain Pray, who has a beautiful ranch, residence and saw mill on the shore." (*San Francisco Daily Alta California*, July 1, 1865. See **China Gardens**, **Glenbrook**, and **Montreal Canyon**.)

Lucille, Lake   California: El Dorado
Echo Lake

Named for Lucille Meredith, whose husband was a banker in Oakland about 1900. (USFS.) The name appeared on the Forest Service quad in 1945 and the *Fallen Leaf* 15-minute quad, 1955.

Luther Pass   California: El Dorado
Freel Peak

Named for Ira Manley Luther (1821–1890), who came to California in 1850. The exact year is established in a letter dated May 13, 1857 from Sherman Day, surveyor in 1855 of the State Immigrant Wagon Road. He wrote from the New Almaden Mine: "Mr. Luther, of Sacramento, passed through the Pass over the eastern summit with a wagon in 1854, and painted his name upon a rock; and hence I named it Luther's Pass. Mr. Henderson, Mr. Cary and others made a hasty reconnaissance of it in the winter of 1854–'55, and in the Fall of that year, after examining several other routes, I selected it as the most central and desirable point to cross into Carson Valley, and proceeded to locate the route in detail by a careful instrumental survey. To distinguish it from Johnson's route, I have usually called it 'the Luther's Pass route.'" (*Sacramento Daily Union*, October 8, 1855. See **Johnson Pass**.)

George H. Goddard crossed Luther Pass in 1855. "From this point we ascended the valley about a mile further, and crossed over in a south-easterly direction from Lake Valley, through Luther's Pass, into Hope Valley, at the head of Carson Cañon, distance about six miles. Mr. Luther, of Sacramento, first crossed this pass with a wagon in 1854. It was surveyed during last winter by Mr. Henderson, County Surveyor of El Dorado County, as a portion of the route from Placerville by way of the South Fork, to Cary's Mill. This pass is, naturally, one of the best I have seen over this range of mountains. Several miles of it are now good natural road. The other portions need grading, and removal of rocks. For about a mile the upper portion of the valley through which the pass opens, is occupied by a lagoon and marshy flat [Grass Lake]." (Goddard, *Report*, 80. See **Grass Lake**.)

In a letter dated October 5, 1855, Goddard wrote: "By following the new pass, now called Luther's pass, from Bigler Lake Valley to Hope Valley, the descent is made easy, could the narrow valley between the Johnson pass and Luther's pass be bridged over, by a lofty viaduct, of all the routes yet known, this would be the one for the Pacific Railroad, as there need be no grade upon it, exceeding 100 feet to the mile." (*San Francisco Daily Evening Bulletin*, October 8, 1855. See **Lake Valley**.) "Luther's Pass" appeared on Goddard's map, *Sierra Region South of Lake Tahoe*, and on Hoffmann's 1873 map.

According to Maule, Arthur Brockliss, an early resident, stated that Luther owned a ranch adjacent to Olds Road, and operated a small water-powered sawmill from 1858 to 1865 near the mouth of a canyon that lies south of Jobs Peak in Nevada, and is named Luther Canyon. "GLO plat of T. 12 N, R. 19 E, surveyed in 1862 shows undoubtedly the site of the mill in Section 35, as well as roads and site of Luther's squatter ranch in Section 25 & 26 in the same township." (Maule, 9, 22, 40.) Luther served as a delegate to the Second Nevada Territorial Legislature in 1861 and 1862.

On April 3, 1860 the first Pony Express rider left San Francisco for St. Joseph, Missouri, following the road through Sacramento, Placerville, Johnson Pass, Lake Valley, over Luther Pass, down West Carson Canyon, past Woodford's, along the base of the Carson Range to Genoa and Carson City, and on east.

"Later From The Boundary Survey. A member of the Eastern Boundary Commission, writing from Luther's Ranch, Carson Valley, August 23d, gives the following interesting account of the progress of the survey southward from Lake Valley: . . . The mountains over which we had traveled were so exceedingly rough that it was impossible for a mule to get over, and we had sent the entire train, with K., over the Kingsbury grade, with instructions to stop at Luther's ranch. Consequently we were obliged to pack a pair of blankets each, and provisions for two days, at the end of which time we expected to be within connecting distance of the train in Carson valley. Of course we carried with us only what was absolutely necessary to keep us alive. The bill of fare for supper was very simple. Each man gets a stick about two feet long, sharpens both ends; with one end he impales a slice of bacon, sticks the other end in the ground at a proper distance from the fire, cuts a cold biscuit in half, removes a little piece from the center and places it under the bacon to catch the drippings. Bacon, biscuits, and cold water drank from the sole dish brought along by the company constituted the bill of fare; yet, with camp stories and a few wild onions found growing along the banks of the stream, it was enjoyed as much as was ever kingly feast." (*Sacramento Daily Union*, August 27, 1863.) Referring to the surveyors, the narrative went on to mention Mrs. Luther, who said to her husband: "That is not a star which you saw on the top of the mountain [Jobs Peak]; it has not stirred since you first saw it." It was a signal fire. (See **Jobs Sister** and **Kingsbury Grade**.)

McFaul Creek

Nevada: Douglas

Glenbrook
South Lake Tahoe

Named for William McFaul, a wood contractor who split wood in wintertime and pastured dairy cattle during the summer in the meadow lands at Marla Bay. He is said to have cleared the timber at what is now named Al Tahoe. In the 1890s he sold Round Mound to the Dangbergs of Minden. When McFaul died in 1912 the Marla Bay property was sold to the Cogel family. (Scott, 243–44. See **Al Tahoe**, **Marla Bay**, and **Round Mound**.)

McKinney: Bay, Creek, Lake

California: El Dorado, Placer

Homewood

Washoe Indians collected berries and fished in the creeks in this area, which they called "*cu'wE'thUkhwO'tha* (*cu'wE'thUkh*, a kind of berry; *wO'tha*, river). This is the small stream near Chambers Lodge. Besides fishing, the Washo collected *cu'wE'thUkh*, and the following medicinal plants: *damukOkoi*, whose use I do not know; and *bEziEzInthE'khi*, which was used for eye trouble and also for sore throat. Another plant found in this region was *mugaulu*. The Washo believed that the root of this plant had a magical efficacy in deer hunting when used in the proper manner—it put the deer to sleep. Only shamans collected this plant." (Freed, *Washo*, 80–81. See **Chambers Lodge**.)

"Commencing on the shores of Lake Tahoe, the creek that divides Placer County from El Dorado is McKinney's Creek, named for John McKinney, a native of Illinois, I think, an early day miner, hunter and trapper. He is said to have built the first house at Lake Tahoe some time in the 50's. It was a small log cabin and still standing in 1888, but was not occupied. It was on McKinney Creek some distance back from the lake so as to be away from the beaten path of the Indians, whose trail followed the lakeshore. McKinney came to El Dorado County in the early 50's. He mined for a time around Georgetown and Spanish Flat, but his love for the hills caused him to forsake mining for hunting and trapping. He was one of the first to open up a resort on the lake. His hotel known far and wide as McKinney's was on the north side of the creek and wholly in Placer County. It was a popular stopping place in the 80's and 90's, but McKinney was a poor businessman. He became involved and lost his property and died at the County Hospital at Auburn, Placer County, some time in the 90's. There is also a Lake Mc-Kinney named for him, and the bulge in the lake north of McKinney's, or Chambers Lodge as it is known today is McKinney Bay. As a boy in 1888 I was one of a party that camped for a time at Lake Tahoe. One of our party was an old miner that had known McKinney for years. He would sometimes visit with McKinney and I would be along. Mc-Kinney was a tall, rawboned silent man, dressed in a dark suit of good material, light woolen shirt, no necktie, (I doubt if he ever wore one), and he had beaded Indian moccasins on his feet. His coat pockets were stuffed with jerky (dried venison) which he had prepared himself and this he would give out to his friends. I often think that it was the best jerky that I have ever tasted." ("The Knave," *Oakland Tribune*, July 23, 1944.)

Courtesy, California Historical Society, San Francisco
The steamer *Governor Stanford* at McKinney's. Southern Pacific Company photo.

McKinney patented 126 acres in sec. 12, T. 14 N., R. 16 E. on July 20, 1874. The name "McKinney Creek" appeared on the Wheeler map of 1881.

"Soundings were made in Lake Tahoe in November 1875 by Messrs. John McKinney and Thomas Jackson, two of the oldest settlers in this section of California. The apparatus used belonged to the Coast Survey, and was forwarded from Oakland, by Prof. Joseph LeConte. . . . Most of the brooks in this range rise on the ridge-line, flow eastward, and empty into Lake Tahoe, the more prominent of which are Blackwood and McKinney's Creeks. The water of all these streams is cold and clear." (Wheeler, *Report*, 1287, 1291.)

In 1881 the *Tahoe Tattler* reported that J. W. McKinney was as fat and jolly as ever, and happily doing a lively business with twenty cottages all newly painted. In 1887 McKinney married Mrs. Minnie Bates. (Scott, 86.) George T. Murphy recalled: "Old John W. McKinney was as great-hearted a man as you'd ever want to meet, and just as grand to work with." (*Tahoe Tattler*, July 26, 1935.) By the 1890s McKinney's was the "oldest and best known resort on the western shore." (*Sacramento Daily Union*, June 15, 1890.)

"Though a man of practically no education—it is even said by those who claim to have known him well that he could neither read nor write, but this seems impossible—he was a man of such keen powers of observation, retentive memory, ability in conversation and strong personality, that he was able to associate on an equality with men of most superior attainments. John Muir was a frequent visitor to his home, especially in the winter time when all tourists and resort guests had gone away." (James, *Lake*, 319.)

When he returned from a week in "The winter glory of the Sierra!" John Muir wrote: "How little is known of it! Californians admire descriptions of the Swiss Alps, reading with breathless interest how ice and snow load their sublime heights, and booming avalanches sweep in glorious array through their crowded forests, while our own icy, snow-laden mountains, with their unrivaled forests, loom unnoticed along our eastern horizon. . . .

"Every tree is loaded with the fairy bloom, bending down the branches, and hushing the singing of the elastic needles. When the storm is over and the sun shines, the dazzling snow at once begins to settle and shift and fall off the trees in miniature avalanches; then the relieved branches spring up and shake themselves dry, and the whole green forest, fed and refreshed, waves and sings again rejoicing. . . .

"Few even among Californians have any fair conception of the marvelous abundance of glacier lakes hidden in the fastnesses of our mountains. . . . Lake Tahoe is king of them all, not only in size, but in the surpassing beauty of its shores and waters. It seems a kind of heaven to which the dead lakes of the lowlands had come with their best beauty spiritualized. It lies embosomed in mountains of moderate height near the northern extremity of the high portion of the range. . . .

"In summer the woods resound with the outlandish noise of loggers and choppers and screaming mills; skiffs and steamboats skim the lovely blue water in work and play; and ever and anon as you thread the groves along shore you come upon groups of gay tourists sauntering about, gathering flowers, or resting luxuriously in the rosiny shade of the pines, some in easy picnic attire, others all ribbons and colors, glaring wildly amid the green leaves and frightening the wondering squirrels and birds. But winter brings rest. At the sight of the first snowflake pleasure-seekers flee as from a plague, the ax leaves the woods, and the kind snow heals every scar.

"In this letter I intended only to say a good word for winter in the mountains, hoping to incite others to come and enjoy it, sketching our excursion to illustrate the ease and comfort with which such snowy winter rambles may be made. . . . We went by rail to Carson, and from there set out by stage for Glenbrook. After ascending on wheels until we reached the snow-line, the driver attached his four horses to a sled, hoping thus to cross the summit, which is less than eight thousand feet high, without much difficulty. . . . Then we made our way on foot over to the lake. Next day, on a small steam-tug, we crossed the lake to McKinney's, on the west shore, where we were at home. Here we spent a few health-giving, delightful days, rowing, bathing, racing at lightning speed on snow-shoes [skis] down a mountain-side back of the house, and slipping about through the solemn, silent woods. Only the eldest of my companions ventured with me on the steep slopes. This was his first experience on snow-shoes, and the several descents he made were the most remarkable specimens of falling locomotion that I have ever had the fortune to witness. In shooting down steep declivities the long sled-runner-like shoes have to be kept parallel with firmly braced limbs. My friend, however, heedless of advice, launched himself in wild abandon, bouncing and diving, his limbs and shoes in chaotic entanglement, now in the snow, now in the air, whirling over and over in giddy rolls and somersaults that would shame the most extravagant performances of a circus acrobat. How original and inimitable he was! Wonderfully refreshing and exhilarating his queer capers must have been; for on coming to rest, with his runaway members divorced and lost, he would quietly gather himself, pick out the snow from his neck and ears, and say with preternatural solemnity, 'This, Muir, is the very poetry of motion.'

"We also spent rare evenings by the huge fire in McKinney's old cabin. The log walls are covered with trophies of the chase, for our host has been a great hunter in his day. Two live pet coons were frolicking on the floor while our grand old host smiled benignly and played with them, the firelight gleaming on his weathered face. How big he seems, thus brought into relief, and what a shadow he casts! The fragrant rosiny fire is the very god of the home. No wonder the old nations, with their fresher instincts, had their fireside gods.

"At last, when a mild snow-storm was blowing, we rowed to the lower end of the lake and completed our excursion by slipping on snow-shoes down the Truckee cañon to the railroad." ("Tahoe in Winter," *San Francisco Daily Evening Bulletin*, April 3, 1878.)

Courtesy, California Historical Society, San Francisco

McKinney's. Photo by R. E. Wood.

In 1892 William Westhoff took over the resort. In 1907 Glenbrook House was dismantled and taken to McKinney's. David Henry Chambers purchased the hotel and cottages in 1920 and renamed it Chambers' Lodge, "an old fashioned mountain inn, but not a dressy place." (Scott, 87–89. See **Chambers Lodge**.)

McKinney Bay was known earlier as "Upson Bay." That name appeared on the von Leicht-Hoffmann map of 1874. Alfred R. Conkling referred to "Upson Bay" in 1876. (Wheeler, *Report*, 1291.) According to Robert H. Watson, Lauren Upson named the bay in the early 1860s for himself after he "blazed" the Georgetown-Lake Bigler pass, which earlier had been a Washoe Indian trail. (Scott, 231, 477. See **Rubicon**.) In 1864 Upson became US Surveyor General for California, and later was the best known editor of the *Sacramento Union*. His son Warren was a Pony Express rider. (*Sacramento Union*, December 12, 1959. See **Meyers**.)

Madden Creek   California: Placer
Homewood
    The creek is named for Dick Madden, a Squaw Valley stampeder who settled on land beside this creek. James mentioned "Dick Madden Creek." (James, *Lake*, 178, 319.)

Courtesy, Jim Hildinger
The former commemorative sign on the higher of Maggies Peaks, 1973.

Maggies Peaks   California: El Dorado
Emerald Bay
    The southernmost of these two peaks was named "Fleetfoot Peak" by Miss Mary McConnell, daughter of Tom McConnell. "I inquired of

several the name of this romantic peak that we had so unceremoniously visited, and was informed that it had no name. The company, by mutual consent, desired me to give it a name. I referred the matter to Captain Dick Barter, who remarked that it should be named in honor of the first lady who visited it. According to this decision Fleetfoot Peak is the name that was agreed upon by Lava Castle Company No. 2, September 13th, 1870." (*Sacramento Daily Union*, October 22, 1870. See **Dicks** and **Idlewild**.) The story of Mary McConnell's adventure appeared in the *Sacramento Daily Union* on October 22 and 29, 1870.

A metal sign commemorating the event was placed on the peak. It read: "Fleetfoot Peak, ascended by Miss Mary McConnell, Sept. 12, 1869." Only recently has the sign disappeared. (Hildinger.) A photo of the sign appeared in George Wharton James' book *Lake of the Sky*. The name Maggies Peaks is possibly related to Miss McConnell. The twin mountains were also known as "Round Buttons" and "Maggie's Mountains." (Scott, 466.)

Margery, Lake   California: El Dorado
Echo Lake

The origin of the name is unknown. It first appeared on the 1945 Forest Service map and on the *Fallen Leaf* 15-minute quad, 1958.

Marla Bay   Nevada: Douglas
South Lake Tahoe

Marla Bay is named for a native Englishman, John *Marley*, a rancher and stockman who preempted 160 acres in the 1860s and began farming. Captain Augustus W. Pray bought Marley's ranch in 1870 for back taxes, and logged it. Pray sold the property to William McFaul who added a two-story house, barns, and a milk house. Norman DeVaux bought the property in 1922, and sold it in 1929 to A. K. Browne of the Singer sewing machine family. (Scott, 243–44.) Marla Bay was formerly also known as "Marla Cove" or "Marlo Cove" before the present name was made official. (USGS, October 27, 1955 and September 26, 1956. See **McFaul Creek** and **Lower Prey Meadows**.)

Marlette: Creek, Lake, Peak   Nevada: Washoe, Carson City
Marlette Lake

Seneca Hunt Marlette (1824–1911), a native of New York and a graduate of Rensselaer Institute as a civil engineer, came to California on the *Helena* via Cape Horn in 1849. In 1855 he became the Surveyor General for California, and later worked as an engineer and Surveyor

General for Nevada. (Guinn, v. 2, 1213–14.) The *California Blue Book* for 1909 gave September 7, 1853 as the date when he was elected, and January 2, 1854 as the day when he took office as Surveyor General for California. Marlette served until January 1856, and during this time surveyed most of the emigrant wagon roads.

Seneca Hunt Marlette.

"We anticipate that a very considerable amount of information will be embodied in the forthcoming reports of the Surveyor General, Mr. Marlette, and of Mr. Senator [Sherman] Day, who has been for several months engaged in an examination of the several routes spoken of for the immigrant road. As there is little probability that anything can be done towards building a road, for want of funds, under the law, before the meeting of the next Legislature, it is to be hoped all the information possible will be laid before that body soon after it meets. (*Sacramento Daily Union*, September 20, 1855.)

Marlette Lake was created by a dam on Marlette Creek, and held water for local sawmills, flumes, and the Virginia City water supply, which was completed in 1875. (Carlson, 164.) "Duane L. Bliss and H. M. Yerington of Glenbrook placed a dirt fill and stone dam across the head of Marlette Basin in the summer of 1872." (Scott, 300. See **D. L. Bliss State Park** and **Glenbrook**.)

Lt. M. M. Macomb wrote: "A main triangulation station was also made and the topography of the range finished as far as possible to the northward. Marlette Lake was likewise visited and surveyed. This little lake is beautifully situated in a basin just west of the main ridge, and considerable interest attaches to it from the fact that it is the source from which the Virginia Water Company intend drawing their supply. It is easily reached by a very fair wagon-road which leaves the stage-road at Spooner's Station, about five-eighths of a mile from the summit. It drains into Lake Tahoe, but by damming its outlet it has been increased to many times its original size. It now measures about one and a half miles in length by half a mile in breadth, with a superficial area approximating to 300 acres. Our barometric observations make its altitude 7,750 feet or 1,548 feet above Lake Tahoe, and high enough above Virginia City and Gold Hill (some 16 miles distant in a straight line) to give a good head there. In order to get the water across the ridge a tunnel is being pierced through the granite rock composing it about 3 miles north of the lake where the ridge is narrowest. This tunnel is in a fair way toward completion, and will have a length of nearly 4,500 feet, with a cross-section of about 6 by 8 feet. The water will be led to its west end by a ditch or flume. On the eastern slope the flume has been built and is in operation, being at present fed by some of the mountain streams of that slope. Pursuing a tortuous course down the mountain-side until a steep slope is reached, the flume discharges its contents into a pipe which descends rapidly until it reaches its lowest point at Lake View, on the low ridge separating Eagle and Washoe Valleys. Following up this ridge for some 5 miles the pipe delivers its waters to a flume which conveys them to their destination, Gold Hill and Virginia." (Wheeler, *Report*, 1280. See **Spooner**.)

Marlette sold his Lake Tahoe lumber and water interests in the 1880s and moved to Southern California. (Guinn, v. 2, 1214.) "Lake Marlette" is shown on the 1875 *Map of the Comstock Area*. "Marlette Peak" and "Marlette's Lake Reservoir" appeared on the Wheeler map of 1881.

Washoe Indians camped on "the little flat where the creek turns west. This stream was considered good for fishing." The Washoe name is given as *phagathsami*. (Freed, *Washo*, 82.)

Martis: Creek, Peak, Valley California: Placer
Martis Peak

When traveling in this area, William H. Brewer of the Whitney Survey wrote: "Timilick Valley, a chasm, with several fine terraces, the upper one a table several miles in extent—once an outlet North to the Truckee—an old lake undoubtedly." (Brewer, *Field Notes*, August 25, 1864.) It is supposed that Martis, for whom the creek, peak, and valley were named, was a rancher in the valley, which lies east of the Truckee River. (Scott, 467.)

"Heizer and Elsasser (1953) reported on 26 sites in their archeological survey of the high Sierras in the vicinity of Lake Tahoe. Two similar yet distinct archeological complexes were seen in the materials from their survey—Martis and Kings Beach. . . .

"These authors suggest (1953, 21) that 'the Martis Complex may have flourished some time in the first two millennia B.C.'" (Price, *Washo*, 81–82.)

Meeks: Bay, Creek California: El Dorado
Homewood
Meeks Bay

There was a Washoe Indian midsummer camping spot for catching fish and collecting berries and seeds where Meeks Creek flows into Meeks Bay. The camp called *ma'yalawO'tha* was below the present highway bridge. Another nearby creek was called *mugaulu'wO'tha*, and was a favorite fishing place of Indians and bears. (Freed, *Washo*, 80.)

The names are given as "Micks Bay" and "Micks Meadow" on the 1874 von Leicht-Hoffmann map. Several Meeks were registered in the county in the 1800s, but none can definitely be connected with the place. There were Stephen and Joseph Meek, Meeks & Company, and Joseph L. Meek, who traveled with Walker in 1833. (Gudde, 197.)

Brothers Stephen Hall Meek and Joseph Meek, early mountain men, may have been the hay-cutter owners of Meeks & Co.

The *Silver Age* of Virginia City gave notice of what was going on at "Bigler Lake and vicinity. . . . There will be about four hundred tons of hay cut in the valley this Fall. On the north side of the lake, Day will cut thirty-five tons; Wallace & Lambo twenty-five. At the outlet and in Squaw Valley, Fish, Ferguson & Co. will cut at least two hundred and forty tons. On the west side Burton & Co. will cut seventy-five tons, and Meeks & Co., twenty-five. Warren & Upton will cut about fifty tons on the east side. Nearly or quite all of this hay can be shipped to Lake Valley by the schooner, and find a ready sale there." (*Sacramento Daily Union*, September 6, 1862.)

The Wheeler Survey *Report* of 1877 used the name "Meigs Bay." In 1888 Fremont Wood wrote: "At Meeks Bay, a remarkable phenomenon takes place in the water, which is worthy of mention. Before the base of Rubicon Range [underwater] it changes from a beautiful sapphire to a deep purple in color, although the surface at the shore again assumes a bright blue." (*San Francisco Morning Call*, September 2, 1888.)

The earliest record of the Division of Geographic Names (1895) listed "Meeks Bay." In 1918 the US Reclamation Service, and in 1930 the US Coast and Geodetic Survey, still used "Meigs Bay." The El Dorado County official map of 1925 and the US Forest Service *El Dorado National Forest* map of 1929 had it as "Meeks Bay." The USGS file dated October 30, 1935 listed Meigs, Meeks, Meek's—and recommended Meeks Bay, because "Talking to old timers I find that . . . it has always been Meeks." The post office was established June 9, 1929, and was named for Stephen H. L. Meeks, a mountaineer, who operated in the area in the 1850s. Oswald Kehlet was the first postmaster. (Salley, 137.)

Meiss Lake   California: Alpine
Caples Lake

Louis Meiss, born January 19, 1823 in Darmstadt, Germany, sailed from Le Havre, France to New York in 1840. He lived for a while in Cole County, Missouri, then crossed the plains and mountains to California "To see what it was all about." In 1852 he returned to Missouri, and brought his parents, brothers, and sisters back with him to California. The family settled in Drytown, Amador County, and started a butcher shop. In 1853 Louis built a brick building with a marble floor, which served as butcher shop and grocery. The family also engaged in ranching and farming, raising livestock for their butcher shop. In 1854 Louis made another trip across the plains to Jefferson City, Missouri, where he married Elizabeth Dorn. (CSL.) Their son Benjamin R. Meiss patented 160 acres in sections 5 and 8, T. 10 N., R. 18 E. on May 8, 1901. This land is one section—approximately one mile—west of Meiss Lake.

The name first appeared on the *Silver Lake* 15-minute quad, 1959.

Meyers   California: El Dorado
Echo Lake

The site of Yank's Station is California Historical Landmark number 708. "Established as a trading post in 1851 by Martin Smith, it became a popular hostelry and stagestop operated by Ephraim 'Yank' Clement on the Placerville-Carson Road. (See **Tallac**.) Pony Express rider Warren Upson first arrived here on the evening of April 28, 1860. Changing ponies, he galloped on to Friday's in Nevada to deliver his mochila to Bob Haslam for the ride to Genoa. Used as a pony remount station until October 26, 1861, it was sold to George D. H. Meyers in 1873, and the name changed to Meyers." (*California*, 111.)

Warren Upson, nicknamed "Weatherproof," rode the toughest run of the entire overland mail route, from Placerville to Carson City. The Carson City Pony Express agent, Bolivar Roberts, was confident that Upson could bring the mail safely through no matter what the weather. Warren Upson died while whaling off the Alaskan coast. (Wells Fargo; Carter, 86.)

"Meyers" appeared on the von Leicht-Hoffmann map of 1874. "Myers" is on the Wheeler map of 1881. On February 20, 1882 Meyers homesteaded 160 acres in secs. 29 and 32, T. 12 N., R. 18 E. He ran a dairy and cattle ranch, and sold timber rights.

Charles G. Celio patented 160 acres in secs. 5 and 8 of T. 11 N., R. 18 E. in 1883. Celio's two sons each homesteaded 160 acres in secs. 21, 27, and 28 of that township in 1900. (BLM.) The Celio family bought out Meyers in 1903. (Scott, 196.) A post office named for Meyers was established on October 6, 1904. Charles Celio was the first postmaster. (Salley, 139.)

In an interview, B. C. Celio recalled the early stagecoach days. "Concord coaches cost approximately $1000 each, 100 were required for the run from Placerville to St. Joseph, Missouri; 6 horses of the best blood were required for each stage. The harness for each cost $150. . . . A change of horses at intervals of 10 miles required only 3 minutes." (*Tahoe Tattler*, July 3, 1936.)

Mill Creek
Nevada: Washoe

Marlette Lake

Walter Scott Hobart, Sr. located a sawmill beside the creek in 1880. Later the Hobart Line railroad (known locally as the Crystal Bay Railroad), ran both ways from Hobart's Mill Creek Sawmill—south to Sand Harbor and northwest to near Second Creek. (Myrick, 425–29. See **Incline**.)

Montreal Canyon
Nevada: Douglas

Glenbrook

The origin of the name is not known, but there is a possible connection with the not too distant Montreal mine or perhaps with certain French-Canadian pioneers, such as Simon Dubois and Michele Spooner. (See **Spooner**.) Alfred R. Conkling wrote: "1. The Montreal mine. The mine is situated about 2½ miles northwest of Carson City. It was first opened in 1870, and has been worked at intervals ever since. A tunnel, several hundred feet long, has been driven in the side of the mountain, above which is still another tunnel 150 feet in length. . . . A small stamping-mill was in course of erection in September, 1876, and eighteen men were working at that time." (Wheeler, *Report*, 1289.) The name was submitted by the Forest Service in 1956. (USGS.)

Monument Peak
California: Alpine, El Dorado

South Lake Tahoe
Nevada: Douglas

Monument Peak is located on the line between Nevada and California, and was used as a triangulation point by the 1863 Kidder–Ives survey of that line. (Maule, 7.) The Wheeler Survey placed the name on the 1878 map.

Mount Rose Quadrangle

The origin of the name is not known with certainty. It may be named for Jacob H. Rose, an early Carson City pioneer, or for Miss Rose Hickman, a friend of Washoe City newspaper editor H. S. Ham. (Davis, *Nevada*, v. 2, 1031.)

Goddard referred to the mountain as "Wasshoo Peak" in 1855. (Goddard, *Report*, 102. See **Washoe County**.)

In 1876 Lt. M. M. Macomb of the Wheeler Survey recorded: "From here we attempted the ascent of Mount Rose, but found it impracticable from the west." (Wheeler, *Report*, 1284.) The name "Rose Peak" appeared on the Wheeler maps of 1878 and 1881. "Mount Rose" is shown on the *Carson* 30-minute map of 1893. (See **Rose Knob**.)

Nevada

"The name comes from the Spanish word meaning 'snowy' or 'snow-covered.'. . . Nevada is formed of the region of country former-ly known as Western Utah. The whole of Utah, prior to its acquisition by the United States, was a portion of the Mexican Department of Alta California. All this vast region was acquired from Mexico under the treaty of Guadalupe Hidalgo, which was consummated in 1848, and which treaty also gave to the United States, California, Arizona, New Mexico, and a part of Colorado. Nevada constituted a Territory in March, 1861, and was admitted to the Union as a State, October, 1864. . . . Previous to its acquisition by the United States, the region now con-stituting the State of Nevada was wholly occupied by tribes of wild In-dians. The country was then known only to a few white men, trappers and Indians traders, whose business at certain seasons led them into what was then almost a *terra incognito*, and which was marked upon the maps of that day as the 'Great American Desert,' or the 'Unex-plored Region.'" (De Quille, *Comstock*, 11–12.)

Observatory Point   California: Placer
Kings Beach

The name survives on a triangulation point rather than as an actual place name. It commemorates the place where philanthropist James Lick of San Francisco contemplated building a million-dollar obser-vatory in 1873. Lick died in 1876 at the age of eighty. Although in his will he had left money for constructing an observatory at this point, the Deed of Trust was revoked and the plan for an observatory was scrapped. (*Nevada State Journal* (Reno), May 4, 1875.)

"The telescope was turned skyward as soon as the darkness came on, and the afternoon's storm had left the atmosphere in excellent condition for astronomical observations. A five-inch glass is very in-significant compared with the mammoth instrument which the Lick donation promises to place upon the point yonder. Yet there are impor-tant facts which a small glass might test . . . . Astronomers have feared that the vapors which rise from the lake might impair the usefulness of the great telescope, and that upper air currents might be passing over the Sierra summits which would still further obstruct the views." ("Scientific Fun on Lake Tahoe," *Sacramento Daily Record-Union*, July 24, 1875.)

"Site of J. Lick's Observatory" appeared on the von Leicht-Hoff-mann map of 1874. Alfred R. Conkling noted in 1876: "Observatory

Point, a V-shaped cape jutting far out into the lake." (Wheeler, *Report*, 1291.) An observatory named for Lick and built in 1888 with his funds stands atop Mount Hamilton near San Jose. (See **Dollar**.)

Ormsby Peak   Nevada: Carson City
Marlette Lake

Major William M. Ormsby was a pioneer and prominent citizen of Carson City. "Two or three houses were next built on the present site of Carson City, but the town was not regularly laid out until 1858, when the land was purchased by Major Ormsby, who gave the place the name it now bears." (De Quille, *Bonanza*, 7.)

In a lengthy article, J. A. "Snowshoe" Thompson disagreed with Major Ormsby's report concerning the trans-mountain routes. "Major Ormsby has mentioned to me that he offered to take a contract on this road for $3,000 per mile, which would, for nineteen miles—the line of snow—amount to $57,000. A road, covered with the timber growing along its sides, which is pine, would not last more than three or four years at the outside, and thus, too, with a great deal of repairing, as the trees would be constantly falling across it, to a greater or lesser extent." (*Sacramento Daily Union*, May 27, 1857. See **Thompson Peak**.)

Smith and Ormsby were agents for the overland stage. "Tracy's Express connecting with Wells, Fargo & Co., is in full operation between Placerville and Genoa, and it is destined to do a large business." (*Sacramento Daily Union*, July 13, 1857.)

In 1857 Ormsby "sent an express, which arrived here this morning, for ammunition, &c., to be ready for an emergency. An Indian war is inevitable, as the frequent murders—saying nothing of robbery—by this tribe [Washoe] calls for prompt action on the part of residents." (*Sacramento Daily Union*, October 5, 1857.) In the same issue another correspondent wrote: "I am also informed that one hundred Pyute Indians and twenty or thirty whites, under the command of Major Ormsby, were to start yesterday in pursuit of the Washoes and Little Valley Indians. . . . Doctor [Daggett] informs me that the Pyute Indians came into Carson Valley, three or four hundred strong, and volunteered to join the whites in a fight against their ancient enemy, the Washoes, the tribe living about here." (Ibid. See **Daggett**.)

Ormsby was killed in May 1860 in the Pyramid Lake Indian War. The newspapers of the time wrote him up as a hero. "Major Ormsby remained behind, calling as long as he was able, for the men to rally and cover the retreat, and save the wounded and those who were un-horsed; but all in vain! It is owing to base cowardice that so many brave men were slain, and the thief, murderer and gambler returned unhurt, while the killed and missing were among the best in society. It was the most disgraceful scene that ever took place in civilized war-fare. Major Ormsby remained on his horse for five or six miles, with his bridle hanging on the animal's neck. He died in his saddle, and pitched forward on his head, falling on the ground." (*Sacramento Daily Union*, June 4, 1860.)

John A. Thompson, who later became famous as "Snowshoe" Thompson, was in the war. In 1876, a few months before he died, Thompson was interviewed by Dan De Quille. "He saw Major Ormsby of Carson City fall. His own horse was shot from under him and on foot he struck out for the Truckee River, the retreat being general and most disorderly. As he ran toward the river a horse ran after him. The frightened animal kept close at his back as though hoping to be pro-tected. A man cried out: 'Why don't you get on that horse that is fol-lowing behind you?' Thompson wheeled about, and as he did so struck his head against the animal's nose. It was a horse all saddled and bridled whose rider had fallen in the fight. Thompson at once mounted and thus got away." (*Virginia City Daily Territorial Enterprise*, February 13, 1876.)

De Quille wrote quite a different version of what actually precip-itated the war. "After the trouble was all over, the cause of it was ascer-tained. It was this: In the absence of Williams, proprietor of the station [Williams Station] where the massacre, as it was called, occurred, two or three men left in charge had seized upon two young Piute women and had treated them in the most outrageous manner, keeping them shut up in an outside cellar or cave for a day or two.

"The husband of one of the women, coming in search of his wife, heard her voice calling him from the place in which she was hidden. When he attempted to go to his wife's assistance the men at the station beat him and drove him away, threatening to kill him if he did not leave at once. It so happened that the women who had been outraged were of the branch of the Piute tribe living at Walker Lake, who had married men of the Bannock tribe. The Indian who was driven away from the station hastened to Walker Lake and informed the chief man there of the outrage, asking him to send a band of braves to punish the men at the station. But the sub-chief at Walker Lake would send no men.

"The wronged Indian then went to old Winnemucca, who said he would send no men, that he wanted no trouble with the whites. His advice was that the whites be informed of the outrage, and requested to punish the men in their own way, in accordance with their laws.

"Not satisfied with this, the Bannock went to young Winnemucca, the war-chief. Here he was given the same advice that he had already received from the old chief. Thirsting for vengeance, the man then hastened to his own country and his own chief.

"When the chief of the Bannocks had heard the man's story, he at once gave him thirty of his best men, and told him to go and avenge the wrong that had been done him. He went, and the result is known.

"After killing the men and burning the station, the Bannocks marked their return trail with blood. They murdered in cold blood several small parties of unarmed prospectors. The bodies of these were not discovered until after the last fight at Pyramid Lake, when the murders were charged to the account of the Piutes. . . . Before the fight began he (young Winnemucca) showed a white flag and wished to explain matters, but a man among the whites, who had a telescope rifle, fired and killed an Indian who showed himself on the rocks, and thus precipitated the battle which ended so disastrously for the whites." (De Quille, *Bonanza*, 81–82. Dan De Quille was remembered by Charles Carroll Goodwin as being "in close rapport with the Indians and Chinese, and they all brought their troubles to him." Goodwin, 214.)

A. W. Hawley wrote, I would "never have permitted my men to be led into such a slaughter pen as Ormsby led them into." (Hawley, 5.)

Osgood Swamp   California: El Dorado
Echo Lake

Neamiah "Nemie" Osgood, a native of New Hampshire, settled in El Dorado County in 1859. Osgood Toll House stood at the foot of Meyers Grade where the outlet creek from Echo Lake flows into the Upper Truckee River. In 1866 Osgood was given the title of superintendent of the Kingsbury-McDonald Toll Road. On October 25, 1871 Osgood patented 160 acres in secs. 30 and 31, T. 12 N., R. 18 E. According to Ralph King, the old log toll station washed off its foundation in the 1910–11 deluge. (Scott, 177, 192, 483.) The Celio family later collected the logs and moved them to their property in Meyers. In 1974 local citizens helped move the building to the proposed historical museum site in the South Lake Tahoe-El Dorado County Campground. (Greuner, 7. See **Meyers**.)

Pacific Crest Trail   California: El Dorado, Placer
Echo Lake
Emerald Bay
Homewood

"A high trail winding down the heights of our western mountains with mile markers and shelter huts—like those pictures . . . of the 'Long Trail of the Appalachians'—from the Canadian border to the Mexican Boundary Line! This idea originated with Miss Catherine Montgomery of Western Washington College in 1926." (Hazard, 57.)

This trail, which would run 1,600 miles from Mexico to Canada, was first promoted by Clinton C. Clarke of Pasadena in 1930. In 1932 Clarke presented the idea of a Pacific Crest Trailway to the Forest Service and Park Service. (Clarke, 15.) In 1969 Congress adopted the trail.

Page Meadows   California: Placer, Washoe
Tahoe City

John and Frances Page grazed dairy cattle on the meadows from 1863 to 1880. (USGS.) Robert H. Watson related the story that John Page was hanged for "slitting a horse's throat, but only after it was discovered he had topped this off by murdering the rider." (Scott, 53, 474.) The name at one time was incorrectly spelled "Paige." (USGS.)

Painted Rock   California: Placer
Tahoe City

Origin unknown. The name appeared on the *Tahoe City* quad, 1955. Painted Rock is a summit on the Tahoe basin boundary about 3.5 miles northwest of Tahoe City.

Paradise Flat   California: El Dorado
Emerald Bay
Meeks Bay

Origin unknown. The name appeared on the 1944 Forest Service map and on the 1955 *Tahoe* 15-minute quad.

Parson Rock   California: El Dorado
Emerald Bay

Called this because it resembles a pulpit. (Scott, 129.)

96

Phipps: Peak, Pass   California: El Dorado
Rockbound Valley

Named for Kentucky native and Indian War veteran General William Phipps, who settled at Georgetown in 1854. ("The Knave," *Oakland Tribune*, July 23, 1944.) In 1860 he built a hand-hewn cabin along the creek—General Creek—also named for him. According to James the creek was also called Phipps Creek. "At the mouth of the creek this pioneer [Phipps] located on 160 acres [July 1, 1869], which, when he died about 1883, was sold to M. H. de Young of the *San Francisco Chronicle*. After holding it for many years he sold it in turn to I. Hellman, the banker, who used it as his summer estate, having built a fine residence upon it." (James, *Lake*, 197–98. See **General Creek** and **Sugar Pine Point**.)

Pioneer Trail   California: El Dorado
Echo Lake
Freel Peak
South Lake Tahoe

In 1859 the Pioneer Trail was the most heavily used route to the Comstock Lode. (Greuner, 9.) "Half a dozen stage-lines were running into the place [Comstock, Virginia City], and these arrived loaded down with passengers—capitalists, miners, 'sports,' thieves, robbers, and adventurers of all kinds." (De Quille, *Bonanza*, 99.) Jared B. Crandall's Pioneer Stage Company and Wells Fargo were among the many stagecoach companies. James M. Crane wrote: "The road is, however, now open between Placerville and Genoa, and from Genoa to Salt Lake. Col. J. B. Crandall has made it a stage road. He is the first man in America who has ever established a stage line to cross the Sierras. He is the pioneer stage man between the Pacific ocean and the Great Basin of the continent. He has made his mark in this respect, and the history of this country cannot trace truthfully the events of this great region of the Globe without blending his name therewith." (*Sacramento Daily Union*, July 13, 1857. See **Echo**.)

"By 1860 a toll wagon road crossed the southern part of the Tahoe Basin on the route of the present Pioneer Trail, crossing the Carson Range at Daggett Pass to the Kingsbury Grade and Genoa in the Carson Valley." (Strong, 14. See **Daggett, Kingsbury Grade**, and **Genoa**.)

Leaving San Francisco on April 28, 1860, the first eastbound Pony Express rider followed the Pioneer Trail east to Carson City. (Greuner, 9. See **Meyers**.)

Placer County   California

According to Sanchez there is no true or one explanation of the name *placer*. In old Spanish the word means a "sea bottom, level and of slight depth of sand and mud or stone." (Sanchez, 304.) In the California gold country the word grew to mean surface mining of a certain type. Placer County was created from portions of Yuba and Sutter counties on April 25, 1851. (Coy, 200–202.)

Pluto, Mount   California: Placer
Tahoe City

The mountain was one of the last volcanoes in the Tahoe region. (Scott, 467.) The name first appeared on the von Leicht-Hoffmann map of 1874. It is from the Greek *Plouton*, "God of the Underworld" in Greek mythology. (Partridge, 505.) The mountain is named for the presence of plutonic rock, which is "thought to have been formed by igneous action at great depths." (Challinor, 238–39.)

Pope Beach   California: El Dorado
Emerald Bay

George A. Pope of San Francisco, (of Pope and Talbot, a shipping and lumbering company), purchased the 1,000-acre property of William F. Tevis at Lake Tahoe for $100,000 in 1923 from the Anglo London and Paris National Bank. (*San Francisco Chronicle*, June 16, 1923.) The Pope family kept a magnificent summer home there, called Vatican Lodge. (*San Francisco Examiner*, September 1, 1953.) In 1950 and 1951 the USFS purchased the Pope and Baldwin estates, including the beaches. (Strong, 83.) A Washoe Indian bedrock mortar site has been located here. (Freed, *Washo*, 82.)

Pyramid Peak Quadrangle

"We continued along the Carson Road, which here bends off considerably to the south-east and descends some 200 feet in the next two miles. This is the low depression in the ridge which is seen at the head of Weber Creek, from Placerville Hill, and over which Pyramid Peak and its group are seen in the distance. Here the Diamond Springs Road branches off on a divide to the south. . . .

"Immediately on starting, our road re-ascended the ridge, at which point we took bearings on Pyramid Peak and several other points. . . .

"The views obtained to the north are very grand; all the creeks falling to the American have broken up the country in the roughest possible manner, while beyond them Pyramid Peak towers aloft, forming a magnificent back ground to one of the most striking scenes on the road." (Goddard, *Report*, 98–100.) "Pyramid Peak" appeared on a Goddard map. (Goddard, *South*.)

"Climbed Pyramid Peak . . . up steep slope to summit. . . . Several pretty little lakes near. . . . The ridges near Lake Tahoe apparently all volcanic." (Brewer, *Field Notes*, August 20, 1863.) "On a strip of wood, many names are carved. Among the rest, the following inscription. 'Pyramid Peak is 9413.1 ft. above the sea. Measured Oct. 19th 1862 by W. W. Harvey, C.E." (Brewer, *Observations*, August 20, 1863.)

Alfred R. Conkling wrote: "I have condensed the following extract from Professor Joseph Le Conte's paper on 'Ancient Glaciers of the Sierra,' as he has studied the glacial phenomena thoroughly: 'Between the Eastern and Western Summits lies a trough fifty miles long, twenty miles wide, and 3,000 to 3,500 feet deep. This trough is Lake Valley. It was formerly occupied by a great glacier rising near Pyramid Peak, filling Lake Tahoe, and escaping northeast toward the plains.'

"The predominating rock in the western summit is granite. But igneous rocks such as basalt, diorite, and phonolite have broken through the granite in several places. This range may be fitly divided into the Pyramid Peak ridge, the Tallac Peak ridge, the Twin Peak ridge, and the ridge north of Truckee Cañon.

"Beginning on the south, the Pyramid Peak ridge consists chiefly of granite. This is the westernmost ridge of the western summit, and its southern boundary is the American Fork Cañon, a narrow, windy valley with precipitous sides composed of gray granite. The peak itself is a mass of coarse-grained, yellowish granite in the form of a pyramid, rising about 300 feet above the ridge-line. The altitude of Pyramid Peak is 10,003 feet. The north side of this peak is much steeper than the other sides. Angular fragments of granite cover the slope of Pyramid Peak for a distance of a quarter to a half a mile from the top. There is a small grass patch on the northeast side of the mountain. The eastern declivity of Pyramid Peak passes gradually into the 'Devil's Basin' [Desolation Wilderness], a vast amphitheater of granite, probably formed by glacial agency, and containing a series of lakelets. A serrated ridge forms the eastern boundary of this basin. The rock is grayish granite, with large, dark specks of the same rock disseminated through it at the point where the Placerville road crosses the western summit [Echo Summit]. At first sight these spots presented the appearance of hornblende, but on close examination it was found that they were only a darker variety of the granite, although the forms were six-sided." (Wheeler, *Report*, 1291–93. See **Desolation Wilderness**.)

Quail Lake   California: El Dorado
Homewood

Origin unknown, but undoubtedly named for the mountain quail that make their summer home in the yellow pine and lodgepole pine belts of the Sierra. (Storer, 265.) Alfred R. Conkling used the name in 1876. "On the northeast side of this mountain [behind McKinney's] is Quail Lake, a body of water having an area of about an acre, and 400 feet above Lake Tahoe." (Wheeler, *Report*, 1294.) The lake served as the water source for McKinney's. (Vernon, 8. See **McKinney**.)

Ralston: Lake, Peak   California: El Dorado
Echo Lake

The peak and the lake are most likely named for William Chapman Ralston (1828–1875), a native of Ohio, who learned the trade of steamboat building and worked on Mississippi River steamers. In 1850 he came to California via Panama, where he was agent for Garrison and Morgan, owners of a line of steamships operating between San Francisco and New York. In 1853 he was promoted as post agent in San Francisco, where the company opened a bank and made him a partner in Garrison, Morgan, Fretz and Ralston. In 1858 the firm became Donahue and Ralston & Co. In 1864 Ralston, with Darius O. Mills and other millionaires, founded the Bank of California. (Hittell, *History*, 552.)

Together with William Sharon and Charles Bonner, Ralston organized the Glenbrook Hotel Co. Later Ralston built the Palace Hotel in San Francisco, which opened after his death. Ralston became president of the Bank of California in 1872, but the bank became insolvent and closed on August 25, 1875. On August 27 Ralston drowned while swimming in the Bay near Black Point [Fort Mason.] (*San Francisco Daily Evening Bulletin*, August 28, 1875.)

The Wheeler Survey showed "Ralston Peak" on the 1881 map. It is not certain if the Wheeler party named it or only noted an existing name.

Red Lake; Red Lake Peak   California: Alpine
Markleeville

Disregarding an Indian's warning, "Rock upon rock—rock upon rock—snow upon snow—snow upon snow. Even if you get over the snow you will not be able to get down from the mountain," Frémont took his large band of men, including Kit Carson and Charles Preuss, with sixty-seven horses and mules (see Appendix 2, 161), and at least

Courtesy, California Historical Society, San Francisco

Charles Preuss, cartographer on Frémont's first,
second, and fourth expeditions to the West.

one dog, across the Sierra in the dead of winter. (Frémont, *Expedition*, 231.) On February 3, 1844 Preuss recorded in his diary: "We are getting deeper and deeper into the mountains and snow." On February 6, "No more salt in the camp. Disgusting." By the 11th: "We are now all snowed in." (See Appendix 2, 156–57.) On February 13 Frémont wrote: "We had tonight an extraordinary dinner—soup, mule and dog." The next day he wrote: "With Mr. Preuss, I ascended to-day the highest peak (10,063 feet) to the right; from which we had a beautiful view of a mountain lake at our feet, about fifteen miles in length, and so entirely surrounded by mountains that we could not discover an outlet." (Frémont, *Expedition*, 234.) Preuss did not mention seeing the lake, but did mention the climb in his diary. (Appendix 2, 160.)

From this peak (Red Lake Peak) Frémont and Preuss were the first white men known to have seen Lake Tahoe. (See **Tahoe, Lake**.) Farquhar thought that Stevens Peak was the mountain from which Frémont and Preuss first sighted Tahoe, but he was convinced by Vincent P. Gianelli's well-reasoned article, "Where Frémont Crossed the Sierra Nevada in 1844," published in the *Sierra Club Bulletin*, October 1959. (Farquhar, *Sierra*, 56, 62.)

"On a small bench of the hill below, and at the foot of Red Mountain, is a small marshy lake, apparently drying up. This is Red Lake." (Goddard, *Report*, 105.) Goddard's map, *Sierra region south of Lake Tahoe*, showed "Red Mountain north of Carson Pass." (Goddard, *South*.) The name "Red Lake" appeared on Reed's map, 1864. The mountain was later renamed for the lake, becoming "Red Lake Peak."

Rockbound Quadrangle   California: El Dorado
The first use of this quadrangle name was for "Rock Bound Lake" on the *Pyramid Peak* 30-minute map, 1889. After a fall snow storm in 1915, the US Forest Service hired Joe Minghetti, a Swiss stone mason, to build the Rockbound Pass Trail, which was to be used by cattle only in an emergency. (Wood, 23.)

Cornelius Beach Bradley and professors Frederick Slate and Henry Senger toured the Lake Tahoe region in the summer of 1895. "Turning here to the left, and following a blind trail along the strike of the ledges, we presently came upon Rockbound Lake, a fine piece of water, with the clear-cut setting which its name suggests." (Bradley, 318.) The name "Rockbound" also applies to a lake, a pass, and a valley.

Rose Knob; Rose Knob Peak   Nevada: Washoe
Mt. Rose

The Rose Knob features are named for Mt. Rose. (Carlson, 205. See **Mount Rose Quadrangle**.) In 1968 the USFS confirmed the use of the name "Rose Knob," but was unable to learn anything from local people about the origin of the name "Mount Rose."

Round Lake   California: Alpine
Caples Lake
Echo Lake

An obvious descriptive name that first appeared on the *Pyramid Peak* 30-minute map, 1889. The lake is on the El Dorado-Alpine county line, near the headwaters of the Upper Truckee River.

Round Mound   Nevada: Douglas
South Lake Tahoe

Earlier this feature was known as "Folsom Peak," for lumberman G. N. Folsom. (Scott, 467. See **Folsom Peak**.) The USGS recorded the name change on October 27, 1955. The mound is also known as "Round Hill."

Rubicon: Creek, Point   California: El Dorado
Emerald Bay
Rubicon: Lake, Peak
Rockbound Valley
Rubicon Bay
Meeks Bay

Lt. M. M. Macomb noted in his 1876 report that "A good trail, opened some years ago by Mr. McKinney, runs from here to Georgetown, crossing a branch of the Middle Fork of the American some eight miles from McKinney's, and called by him the Rubicon." (Wheeler, *Report*, 1282.) The name is taken from the Rubicon River, which is the ancient boundary between Cisalpine Gaul and Italy. Julius Caesar crossed that river to attack Pompey in 49 B.C. Thus the phrase "to cross the Rubicon" means to commit oneself irrevocably. (Partridge, 574.)

The trail runs from behind McKinney's to Georgetown. The Washoe Indians traveled this route over the Sierra to the western foothills to gather acorns and hunt deer. Rubicon Springs was a camping place where they drank from the springs for medicinal purposes.

"Rubicon Point" was on the von Leicht-Hoffmann map of 1874. The name "Rubicon," for the river, appeared on the Hoffmann map of 1873.

"Rubicon Creek" was on the Wheeler map of 1878. "Rubicon Peak" was first named on the Wheeler map of 1881.

Rubicon soda water from Rubicon Springs was bottled and carried out by the Hunsucker brothers. The *Tahoe Tattler* on September 2, 1881 advertised: "Rubicon soda water better than whiskey. Call for a drink."

A post office was established at Rubicon (on Rubicon Bay) on May 4, 1901. (Salley, 190.) James referred to Rubicon Bay as "Grecian Bay." "There is one especially color-blessed spot. It is in Grecian Bay, between Rubicon Point and Emerald. Here the shore formation is wild and irregular, with deep holes, majestic, grand and rugged rocks and some trees and shrubbery. . . . These objects and conditions all combine to produce a mystic revelation of color gradations and harmonies, from emerald green and jade to the deepest amythestine or ultra-marine. . . . The eyes are dazzled with iridescences and living color-changes . . . as exquisite, glorious and dazzling as revealed in the most perfect peacock's tail-feathers, or hummingbird's throat. . . . The blue alone is enough to impress it forever upon the observant mind." (James, *Lake*, 4–5.)

The D. L. Bliss State Park, established in 1932, includes Rubicon Point and Emerald Bay. (Strong, 86. See **D. L. Bliss State Park**.)

Sand: Harbor, Point   Nevada: Washoe
Marlette Lake

The name derives from the beautiful sand beaches that adorn the water's edge. For the Washoe Indians the area served "as a resting spot and not as a full-fledged camping site." (Freed, *Washo*, 82.)

Walter Scott Hobart, Sr. and Walter Scott Hobart, Jr. held 10,000 acres, and during the lumbering days built a railroad, completed in 1880, from Sand Harbor to Incline. (Strong, 29. See **Incline**.) In 1938 "George Whittell owned all the Nevada lake shorelands from Cal-Neva to Glenbrook and four miles south of Glenbrook, including Cave Rock." (*Tahoe Tattler*, July 8, 1938. See **Skunk Harbor**.) Sand Harbor State Recreation Area, created in 1958, was the first state park on the Nevada shore. (Strong, 91.)

Saxon Creek   California: El Dorado
Freel Peak
South Lake Tahoe

The origin of the name is not known. Saxon Creek originates at Freel Meadow and flows northerly, emptying into Trout Creek. It is possible that the name comes from the lumbermen Augustus H. and

Rube Saxton, who operated a sawmill at Ward Creek Canyon on the north shore. (See **Freel Peak, Trout Creek,** and **Ward Creek.**)

Scott Peak   California: Placer
Tahoe City

The origin of the name is not known, but it could be named for the Scott family, who settled in Squaw Valley in 1880, ran a dairy, and later built Deer Park Springs Inn. (Scott, 19–21.) "Scott Peak" first appeared on the *Tahoe* 15-minute map of 1955.

Second Creek   Nevada: Washoe
Marlette Lake
Mt. Rose

This is the second creek one crosses when going from Stateline Point to Incline. (**See Crystal Bay, First Creek, Incline, Stateline Point, and Third Creek.**)

Secret Harbor; Secret Harbor Creek   Nevada: Carson City
Marlette Lake

Origin unknown. Secret Harbor is between Deadman Point and Sand Point.

Shadow Lake   California: El Dorado
Rockbound Valley

The origin is not known. Perhaps the lake received its name because in the early morning it is in the shadow cast by Rubicon Peak, half a mile due east. The lake lies between Crag Lake and Stony Ridge Lake. The outlet stream from Shadow Lake flows into Meeks Creek five miles above Meeks Bay. The name appeared on the *Fallen Leaf* 15-minute quad of 1955 and the Forest Service map of 1945. (See **Rubicon, Crag Peak, Stony Ridge Peak,** and **Meeks.**)

Shakespeare Rock   Nevada: Douglas
Glenbrook

"It was first noticed in 1862 by the wife of Rev. J. A. Benton, of California, who was at that time sketching the mountains." (Angel, *Nevada*, 381.)

C. F. McGlashan wrote: "Tourists passing Glenbrook should always look at Shakespeare's likeness on the granite cliffs that frown above the little village. Standing out in bold relief against the stone-colored rock, is a deep stain that strangely enough forms a perfect likeness to the great bard. Among a hundred observers not one would fail to detect the resemblance and recognize the portrait." (*Sacramento Daily Union,* May 29, 1875.)

The name "Shakespeare Cliff" appeared on the Wheeler map of 1878. Lt. M. M. Macomb described it: "One of the first objects to strike the eye after reaching Glenbrook is a prominent mass of basalt just to the south, which bears the interesting name of Shakespeare's Cliff. A moment's careful inspection will show on an almost vertical escarpment not far from the summit a mass of greenish-gray lichens standing out plainly against the dark surface of the rock. A glance at this will without any stretch of the imagination transform it into a truly striking resemblance to the head and bust of the great poet as seen in profile; the high forehead, massive brows, and pointed beard wonderfully reproduced." (Wheeler, *Report,* 1279.)

Writers and poets took pleasure in this natural wonder. Dan De Quille wrote: "The Shakespeare Rock, plainly visible from the Glenbrook House, on the southern shore of the lake, is so called on account of there being in the rugged outlines of its face a striking resemblance to the features of the immortal poet. All who visit the lake desire first of all to see this rock. Like many other things of the kind, there is much in the position from which it is viewed, and not a little in the imaginative powers of the person viewing it." (De Quille, *Bonanza,* 317.)

Poet, writer, and later San Francisco librarian John Vance Cheney arrived in California in the 1870s. His description reads: "The likeness needs no aid from the imagination; it is life-like, recognized instantly by the most careless observer, and let it be added, never forgotten. The beard is a trifle longer than we are accustomed to see it, but this does not detract from the majesty of expression. . . . The portrait looks as if it were made by moss growing upon the smooth flat surface of a huge rock; but we were informed that it was all of stone." (Rider, 275–76.)

Showers Lake   California: Alpine
Caples Lake

The origin of the name is unknown. It appeared on the *Silver Lake* 15-minute map, 1959. The lake is just north of the Pacific Crest Trail, about a mile east of Little Round Top.

Sierra House   California: El Dorado
South Lake Tahoe

Robert Garwood Dean built Sierra House during 1858 and 1859 on Pioneer Trail beside Cold Creek. Soon after, he sold it to William Mack of Sacramento. Sierra House was one of the more popular inns along the Placerville-Carson Valley back road. (*Sacramento Daily Union*, February 5, 1870.)

"William Mack, late of this city, has built an excellent house, barns, stables, etc., for the accommodation of the public. He has also furnished it with everything necessary for comfort, bought and hauled from Sacramento." (*Sacramento Daily Union*, November 16, 1860.) The name "Sierra Ho." appeared on the Wheeler map of 1881. Charles E. Boles, alias Charles E. Bolton, who used the nickname "Black Bart," robbed the Wells Fargo stagecoaches twenty-eight times between 1875 and 1883; he is said to have stayed at the Sierra House. Disguised by a flour-sack mask, he sometimes left poetry for his victims. (Hart, 42.) The USGS reported that the building was torn down in 1954. Sierra House School, across from the location of the old Sierra House, has lobby walls panelled with wood salvaged from the remaining structures. "It provides an attractive and suitable backdrop for a display of historic pictures and artifacts, many of which were found on the site." (Greuner, 19.)

Courtesy, California Historical Society, San Francisco

The Sierra House, on Pioneer Trail.

Sierra Nevada

Padre Pedro Font was the chaplain and cartographer on Juan Bautista de Anza's second expedition. On April 2, 1776 Font saw and described the Sierra from a hill near the present city of Antioch. "Looking to the northeast we saw an immense treeless plain into which the water spreads widely, forming several low islets; at the opposite end of this extensive plain, about forty leagues off, we saw a great snow-covered mountain range [*una gran sierra nevada*], which seemed to me to run from south-southeast to north-northwest." (Teggart, 85.) Font prepared a map in 1776 on which he had the descriptive words "Sierra Nevada," for the distant snowy mountain range.

"The primary meaning of the Spanish *sierra* is saw, and the term is applied to high mountain chains, the comb or edge of which, seen from a distance, suggests saw teeth. As it would be improper to say 'the Rocky Mountain chains,' so it is improper to say 'the Sierra Nevadas,' or 'the Sierras.'" (Hittell, *Pacific*, 38.)

"This SIERRA is part of the great mountain range, which, under different names and with different elevations, but with much uniformity of direction and general proximity to the coast, extends from the peninsula of California to Russian America. . . .

"That part of this range which traverses the ALTA CALIFORNIA is called the *Sierra Nevada*, (Snowy Mountain)—a name in itself implying a great elevation, as it is only applied, in Spanish geography, to the mountains whose summits penetrate the region of perpetual snow. It is a grand feature of California, and a dominating one, and must be well understood before the structure of the country and the character of its different divisions can be comprehended. It divides California into two parts, and exercises a decided influence on the climate, soil, and productions of each." (Frémont, *Geographical*, 6)

Eldorado, or, Adventures in the Path of Empire, written by Bayard Taylor in 1849, described the mountains: "The afternoon of the second day the clouds lifted, and we saw the entire line of the Sierra Nevada, white and cold against the background of the receding storm. As the sun broke forth, near its setting, peak after peak became visible, faraway to north and south, till the ridge of eternal snow was unbroken for at least a hundred and fifty miles. The peaks around the head-waters of the American Fork, highest of all, were directly in front. The pure white of their sides became gradually imbued with a rosy flame, and their cones and pinnacles burned like points of fire. In the last glow of the sun, long after it had set to us, the splendor of the whole range, deepening from gold to red, from rose to crimson, and fading at last into an ashy violet, surpassed ever the famous 'Alp-glow,' as I have seen it from the plains of Piedmont [Italy]." (Taylor, vol. 1, 231.)

Skunk Harbor   Nevada: Carson City
Marlette Lake

The name of this small bay north of Deadman Point is derived from the animal, *Mephitis mephitis*, which is known to inhabit the Tahoe Basin lands. (Storer, 353.) George Whittell built a stone summer lodge here in the late 1930s. (See **Sand Harbor** and **Deadman Point**.)

Slaughterhouse Canyon   Nevada: Carson City
Glenbrook
Marlette Lake

The origin is not known, but the name suggests that pioneers may have taken livestock into the canyon for slaughtering. (Carlson, 218.) The USGS reported in 1956 that the name was submitted as two words, but the preferred spelling is in use.

Snow Lake   California: El Dorado
Emerald Bay

Snow Lake was formerly called "Katrine Lake" for Katherine Brigham Ebright, the youngest daughter of Dr. Charles Brigham of the Cascade Lake property. (Scott, 141. See **Cascade Lake**.) The lake is at the southern headwaters of Cascade Creek, 1.3 miles southwest of Cascade Lake.

South Camp Peak   Nevada: Douglas
Glenbrook

In 1876 the Carson & Tahoe Lumber & Flume Company's south wood camp was located on the west slope of the peak; hence the name. (Scott, 467.)

South Lake Tahoe (Community)   California: El Dorado
Emerald Bay
South Lake Tahoe

In the middle 1850s what is now called "State Line" was the location of William W. "Billy" Lapham's Hotel and Landing. The name "Laphams" is on Goddard's earliest map. (Goddard, *Sierra*.)

In 1965 voters of the south shore California communities of Tahoe Valley, Al Tahoe, Bijou, and Stateline decided to unite as the city of South Lake Tahoe. It was hoped that some of the beauty and alpine quality of the area could still be saved from the rampant, unplanned development being permitted by the county. The first mayor of the new city, W. Brad Murphy, pledged himself to block further "hodgepodge" urbanization. Land developers, realtors, and gambling interests have prevailed, and growth continues to be the pivotal question. (Strong 125–26.) The South Lake Tahoe post office opened March 24, 1967. (Salley, 209.)

South Point   Nevada: Douglas
Glenbrook
    The namer is unknown. The point is just south of Glenbrook—hence the name. (See **Glenbrook**.)

Courtesy, Nevada Historical Society

At Spooner's Station, October 9, 1889.

Spooner: Junction, Lake, Summit   Nevada: Douglas
Glenbrook
    "Winding along the south slope of this hill is a splendid wagon road leading to several saw mills and a fine body of timber above, and thence over the east summit to Lake Bigler. This road, commenced over a year ago by Mr. Walton, long engaged in teaming and packing into this region, besides having an easier grade, is several miles shorter than the famous Kingsbury road, which it will, for the present, intersect in Lake Valley." (*Sacramento Daily Union*, July 6, 1861.)

Township Lines, surveyed by I. J. Lawson and B. Ives in 1861, shows "M. E. Spooner," "Spooner & Co.'s House," "Lake Bigler Lumber Co.'s sawmill," and a road from Lake Bigler to Carson City.

Lt. M. M. Macomb mentioned the stage-road at Spooner's Station in 1876. (Wheeler, *Report*, 1280.) Conkling reported: "A strip of productive land extends back from the lake for a distance of 2 miles, where it is called Spooner's Meadow." (Wheeler, *Report*, 1289.) Now, due to a dam, it is known as Spooner Lake. Spooner's Junction is at the intersection of Highways 50 and 28.

Stanford Rock   California: Placer
Homewood

Named for California's "Civil War Governor" (1862–63) Leland Stanford (1824–1893). Before coming to California in 1852 to join his five brothers in their retail grocery business, Stanford had worked and studied law in Wisconsin. He was a staunch Union supporter, and founder of the Republican Party in California. Later, as president of the Central Pacific Railroad (one of the "Big Four"), he drove the "Gold Spike" at Promontory Point, Utah on May 10, 1869. In memory of his son, who died at age fifteen, he and his wife established and endowed Stanford University in 1885.

According to Gudde, Professor Bolton C. Brown, who made the first recorded ascent of the 8,743 foot mountain, in August 1896, named it Mount Stanford for the University. Since there was already a Mount Stanford in Placer County, named by the Whitney Survey, its name was changed to Castle Peak. (Gudde, 319.) There is another Mount Stanford in the central Sierra Nevada.

Washoe Indian hunters made overnight use of the caves at the foot of Stanford Rock. (Freed, *Washo*, 81.)

Star Lake   California: El Dorado
Freel Peak
South Lake Tahoe

The name first appeared on the *Markleeville* 30-minute map of 1936. Al Tahoe obtains a portion of its water supply from the lake. (Scott, 210.) "Star Lake played an important part in the early timbering activities of the Tahoe region. Its outlet was controlled to feed a flume which ran from the meadow to the railroads near Sierra House. A portion of the dam and gates can still be seen." (*Tahoe Tattler*, July 2, 1937. See **Al Tahoe** and **Sierra House**.)

Stateline (Community)   Nevada: Douglas
South Lake Tahoe

"No Californian will regret to hear that the new United States survey of the boundary line between California and Nevada gives our
State a large portion of Lake Tahoe heretofore included within the
dominion of Nevada. The line strikes singularly at Lake Valley. It goes
through H. H. Parkell's hotel there, leaving one-half of the dining-
room in the State of California and throwing the other half into the
State of Nevada. One may therefore give an order for food in the one
state and have it executed in the other." (*San Francisco Daily Evening
Bulletin*, July 15, 1873.)

Stateline fronts on the bay between Bijou and Round Mound
(known locally as Round Hill), which earlier was known as "Sapphire
Bay" and "Boundary Bay." (Scott, 241, 487.) The name "Boundary Bay"
is on the Wheeler map of 1881. For years the town, a well-known gambling resort at the south end of Lake Tahoe on the border of California
and Nevada, has remained unincorporated.

"Voters in several resort communities decided yesterday against
forming the city of Lake Tahoe, a move opposed by casinos but favored
by residents demanding more for their taxes.

"The vote was 1,001 against and 802 for the plan.

"The proposed city, with a population of about 6,500, would have
embraced the casino area of Stateline and smaller communities along
about 15 miles of Lake Tahoe's southeastern shore." (*San Francisco
Chronicle*, May 25, 1988. See **Zephyr Cove**.)

Stateline: Point, Lookout   California: Placer
Kings Beach
Marlette Lake

Lt. M. M. Macomb wrote in 1877: "Camp was then moved [from
Martis Valley] to Hot Springs, near the extremity of the promontory
known as State Line Point. This is one of the most interesting places on
the lake, and the view is exceedingly beautiful, especially at this season, when the mountain peaks, capped with snow, contrast strongly
with the dark pine forests clothing their rugged sides. For the accommodation of tourists, a hotel and a number of small cottages have been
erected, the water of the Springs being utilized for bathing purposes.
The proprietor received us with true California hospitality, tendering
us free use of the cottages and baths, which kindness we were glad to
take advantage of, while here the survey of the lake was completed,
and connection made with the monuments of the California and

Nevada State line." (Wheeler, *Report*, 1282.) "Stateline Pt." appeared on the Wheeler map of 1878.

"BACK FROM THEIR WORK. Boundary Line Surveyors Report Their Progress. The State boundary line party of the United States Coast and Geodetic Survey has returned from its season's labors in the Lake Tahoe region.

"C. H. St. Clair says the great system of triangulation, which is being run from ocean to ocean, was utilized in running their lines. Since July they have worked altogether on the upper end of their line, one hundred and twentieth meridian and the thirty-ninth parallel, which occurs right on the lake. Last May they worked on the lower end, 400 miles distant, at the intersection of the thirty-fifth parallel and the Colorado River.

"The first line was run from Yolo to Round Top. Considerable topographical work was done also south of the lake, in the neighborhood of Bijou, Rowland and Tallac.

"Quite a number of distance marks—stone monuments—were established. The boundary line as run is about 100 yards northeast of Von Schmidt's line run in 1873, and about 100 yards this side of the Minto and Grunsky line, which was run in 1889." (*San Francisco Daily Morning Call*, November 4, 1893.)

The boundary line between California and Nevada—from Lake Tahoe to the Oregon state line—has been and continues to be unresolved. Francois D. Uzes charted five different survey lines, beginning with Higley in 1860 west of Kings Beach; Houghton & Ives in 1863 east of Kings Beach; von Schmidt in 1872, considered the present border; Grunsky & Minto in 1889 along the eastern shore of Stateline Point; and the US Coast & Geodetic Survey of 1893 just east of Stateline Point. "In summary, it has been shown that there is at present no accurate survey of the portion of the eastern boundary from Lake Tahoe to Oregon. The 120th meridian was adopted by Congress in 1850 as the state boundary, and no action has been taken by that body to cause a change. The apparently correct location of the meridian is stated to be 1,727 feet east of the posted location at Stateline Point on Lake Tahoe. Neither state has officially sanctioned the posted and monumented 1872 Von Schmidt line, but both apparently utilize it for all governmental purposes. Facilities such as gambling casinos (legal only in Nevada) were built in reliance of this being the true and correct location of the state boundary." (Uzes, 88, 95–96.)

The lookout is situated atop a high point with an altitude of 7,017 feet. It is on the north shore, close to Stateline Point.

Lieutenant Montgomery Meigs Macomb, in charge of the
Wheeler Survey field party of 1876.

Stony Ridge Lake   California: El Dorado
Rockbound Valley

The lake's name is most likely derived from its location between Rubicon Peak and the mountain ridge forming the Tahoe Basin boundary. A dam constructed by the California Youth Authority was completed in 1949. The lake was also known as "Upper Tallant Lake" of the "Tallant Group." (DFG.) The lake drains into Meeks Creek.

Sugar Pine Point; Sugar Pine Point State Park   California: El Dorado
Meeks Bay

Named for the presence of the *Pinus lambertiana,* "a magnificent tree with large cones hanging at the ends of its spreading branches." (Storer, 145.) Goddard referred to the sugar pine as "the pride of the California forest. This truly magnificent tree becomes, as we continue to ascend, the chief tree of the forest." (Goddard, *Report,* 97.)

The location was originally settled by General William Phipps in the 1860s, and was logged in the 1870s. The name "Sugar Pine Point" was the place where, by an act passed in 1863, the Placer-El Dorado county line met Lake Tahoe. (Coy, 201. See **General Creek**.)

In 1877 Lt. M. M. Macomb mentioned "Sugar Pine Point" in his report, and also placed it on the map of 1878. "Before reaching McKinney's the trail crosses a bold projection known as Sugar Pine Point, from the fine trees of that name growing there. A large lumber-camp located here afforded a good opportunity of witnessing the mode of lumbering generally in vogue on the lake. The trees are sawed instead of cut down and converted into saw-logs as they lie. These logs vary from 20 to 60 inches in diameter, the length varying to suit the purchasers, generally between 20 and 30 feet. Perhaps the most interesting feature is the great wagons on which the logs are hauled to the lake. These are made immensely strong, the wheels being constructed of a section cut from a saw-log, and are from 3 to 3½ feet in diameter, being about 6 inches broad at the tire, and bulging out at the center. The heavy cross-beams on the wagon-body are furnished with iron stirrups of peculiar construction, in which rest the ends of heavy planks used in loading. The wagons are drawn by six or eight yoke of oxen. To give an idea of what can be done by these wagons it is a matter of record that 14,900 odd feet of lumber in the shape of saw-logs has been placed upon one of them. This was popularly known as the 'boss load,' and photographs of it can be obtained at Truckee." (Wheeler, *Report,* 1281–82. See **General Creek** and **Mckinney**.)

After the lumbering days, Sugar Pine Point became a favorite resort area, featuring Lapham's Hotel Bellevue (1888–1893).

"The most attractive looking building on [the west] side of the lake is the Bellevue, at Sugar Pine Point. It is three stories high, the rooms are spacious and lofty and very handsomely painted. The wharf is solidly constructed and at the outer end is a handsome saloon and billiard room, with several sleeping apartments in the upper story. Mr. Kaiser has fourteen row and sail boats already constructed which will be a great assistance to the future prosperity of the hotel, as he intends charging no hire for them. The hotel commands the best view of any of the lake shore, and in a year or two when the outlying grounds shall be properly arranged the Bellevue will be the grand resort." (*Truckee Republican*, April 18, 1888.)

Summer homes were built by San Franciscans M. H. de Young of the *San Francisco Chronicle* and I. W. Hellman of the Nevada Bank and later of the Wells Fargo Bank. "Last week M. H. Deyoung, proprietor of the San Francisco *Chronicle*, made an extensive purchase of real estate at Tahoe. Evidently he has great faith in the future of the place as a summer resort and is already using the columns of his paper to assist in getting up a boom." (*Semi-Weekly Truckee Republican*, August 20, 1887.)

Walter D. Bliss designed both the Tahoe Tavern and the Hellman's Tahoe home, which was completed in 1903. By 1913 Hellman had acquired 2,021 acres. (Hart, 182.) In 1965 Sugar Pine Point State Park was established when the state purchased 1,975 acres—including the Hellman summer residence and 7,700 feet of lake frontage—for $8.3 million, and added another thirty-six acres the next year. The gracious beachfront Hellman home is open to the public. (Strong, 26, 88.)

Sunnyside (Community)   California: Placer
Tahoe City

The community is named for the resort developed by Mrs. Hayes in the early 1880s from the site of Saxton's old mill and wharf. Her resort included cottages, a boathouse, and a pier. Although the names are no longer in use, the bay was once called "Hurricane Bay," and was later named "Sunnyside Bay" by Mrs. Hayes. (Scott, 59, 475.)

Susie Lake   California: El Dorado
Emerald Bay
Rockbound Valley

There are two explanations for the name. Scott suggests that it was named for Susan Gilmore, the oldest daughter of Nathan and

Amanda Gilmore. (Scott, 150. See **Gilmore Lake** and **Glen Alpine**.)
Robert S. Wood suggests that it was named for Susie—the matriarch
among the Washoe Indian squaws who came up from Carson Valley as
recently as the 1920s and camped for the summer at Lake Tahoe.
(Wood, 21.) A photograph of "Susie, the Washoe Indian Basketmaker,
and Narrator of Indian Legends" appears in *Lake of the Sky*. (James,
Lake, 408.) The USGS field investigation of 1955 confirmed the spelling
of "Susie" rather than "Suzy," as it appeared on all editions of the
Pyramid Peak 30-minute map, 1889–1954. (See **Red Lake**.)

Tahoe, Lake   California and Nevada
On February 14, 1844 John Charles Frémont and Charles Preuss "ascended to-day the highest peak to the right [Red Lake Peak]; from
which we had a beautiful view of a mountain lake at our feet, about
fifteen miles in length, and so entirely surrounded by mountains that
we could not discover an outlet." (Frémont, *Expedition*, 234.) In his
report published in 1845, Frémont called the lake "Mountain Lake."
"L. Bonpland" appeared on Frémont and Preuss's 1848 *Map of Oregon
and Upper California*, and on an 1849 French map, *Carte de la haute
California, d'apres les plans du capitaine Frémont*. (Bancroft Library.) The
name was in honor of the French botanist Aimé Jacques Alexandre
Bonpland (1772–1858), companion of Alexander von Humboldt (1769–
1859), the German naturalist, explorer, and statesman. Frémont and
Preuss are considered to be the first white men to have seen Lake
Tahoe.

"In Wilkes' map and others, published about the period of the gold
discovery, it bears the former name [Mountain Lake]. When Col. Johnson laid out his road across the mountains, the lake passed unnoticed
except under the general term of Lake Valley. Gen. Winn's expedition,
or the emigrant relief train, first named it Lake Bigler, after our late
Governor [John Bigler]. Under this name it was first depicted in its
transmountain position in Eddy's State map, and thus the name has
become established." (*Sacramento Daily Union*, August 31, 1857.)

Colonel J. C. Johnson, a resident of Placer county, made the first trail
into Lake Valley and Carson Valley, and was credited with the discovery and naming of the lake and Lake Valley. (*Sacramento Daily
Union*, February 2, 1870. See **Johnson Pass** and **Lake Valley**.)

From Carson City in 1851 a Lieutenant Tyffe sent the *Sacramento
Daily Union* "a description of a valley which he examined in company
with Mr. Gleason, who discovered the valley, and gave it his own name
at a previous period.

A portion of the Frémont map of 1845. Lake Tahoe appears
on a map for the first time, but is not named.

"Mr. Tyffe says that on their way to it they ascended a range of
mountains on the west of Carson valley, until they reached the summit.

. . . There was a large lake terminating in [the valley] near the center, from which two streams could be traced up for several miles where they divide off into six or seven smaller ones that irrigated the extremity of the valley which was not overflowed with the lake. The lake was supposed to be about fifty miles in length and from fifteen to twenty miles in width. A great portion of the valley was studded with and nearly surrounded by a heavy growth of pine and cedar trees. Along the eastern side of the lake and valley there was a strip of land upon which a most luxuriant growth of grass appeared and also on a portion of the center of the valley.

"The streams abounded with fish, among which were trout in great plenty. On some of the streams on the western range of the valley they found an Indian settlement which had been recently deserted, and at which there were ingenious Indian contrivances for catching fish." (*Sacramento Daily Union*, September 2, 1851.) Thus for a brief period, the lake and its valley were named "Gleason Valley."

It was reported that the name Lake Bigler "had been recognized by everybody as the name of the lake since 1851, as was well known by all old Californians." (*Sacramento Daily Union*, February 2, 1870.)

The following is an early account of "Lake Bigler. —This is the name given to one of the largest, if not the largest lake in California. It is at least fifty miles long, with an average width of from ten to twenty miles; and yet we look in vain upon 'Trask's New Map' even for its position or locality, although well known to be the great source of the Truckee River. . . . It abounds with fish of several varieties, among which the speckled trout, many of large size, and the salmon, predominate. They are taken in considerable numbers by the Indians that resort to this, their wildly romantic and beautiful summer retreat." (*Auburn Placer Herald*, June 25, 1853.)

"The lake in Col. Frémont's map attached to his Report, is called Mountain Lake, and in the general map by Charles Preuss, Lake Bompland [Bonpland]. It has since been named Lake Bigler, and as such is most generally known. An endeavor has lately been made to name it Truckee Lake, from its being on the head waters of that river, but as a lake lying to the north of the Truckee Pass has been known for many years under that name, it would be very unadvisable to disturb the present names." (Goddard, *Report*, 105.) It should be noted that Frémont apparently did not actually give the name "Mountain Lake" to Lake Tahoe. He simply used those words as a descriptive term: ". . . we had a beautiful view of a mountain lake at our feet. . . ." (See **Red Lake**.)

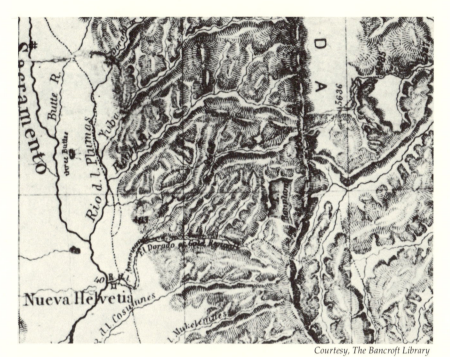

From the Frémont-Preuss map of 1848.
Lake Tahoe has the name L. Bonpland.

"Lake Bigler, unfortunate in name, lies between the western and middle ranges of the Sierra Nevada. It appears to be about as long as the portion of San Francisco Bay, between San Jose and San Francisco, and about twice as wide. . . . A few ducks and an occasional crane or heron are seen along the shores. . . . Where the beach is sandy, the tracks of deer and foxes may be seen, and it was my fortune to observe a solitary Indian hunter, also making tracks in the vicinity." (*San Francisco Daily Evening Bulletin*, August 22, 1857.)

Controversy over the lake's name began to stir in the newspapers. "Among the bills introduced, was one to change the name of Lake Bigler to Tula Tulia, the Indian name of the lake." (*Sacramento Daily Union*, April 13, 1861.)

In the early 1860s William Henry Knight and Henry De Groot compiled the first maps to change "Lake Bigler" to "Lake Tahoe." John S. Hittell, editor of the *San Francisco Daily Alta California*, and Dr. Henry De Groot, correspondent of the *Sacramento Union* and the *San Francisco Bulletin*, met with Knight to discuss the name change. De Groot had made an exploring trip to the lake in 1859 with a Washoe Indian guide,

Courtesy, The Bancroft Library

A portion of Bartlett's map of 1854. Lake Tahoe is now shown as Bigler L.,
but it is placed too far north. There is also a non-existent Mountain L. shown.

and had compiled a list of Washoe names. "He took a memorandum
from his pocket and examined a list of Indian names of which he had
made notes, and exclaimed: 'Why here it is; the Washoe tribe call it
Tahoe, meaning Big Waters." (Knight, 40.) Knight obtained approval
for the use of the name "Lake Tahoe" from the General Land Office,
and all subsequent Department of the Interior maps used that name.
Carl Wheat maintained: "The name Tahoe was proposed sometime in
1862 and thereafter found its way both to De Groot's map and to that
of Knight. . . . We are happy to accord Knight and De Groot joint credit
for applying a fitting name to one of the world's most beautiful lakes."
(Wheat, vol. 5, part 1, 73.)

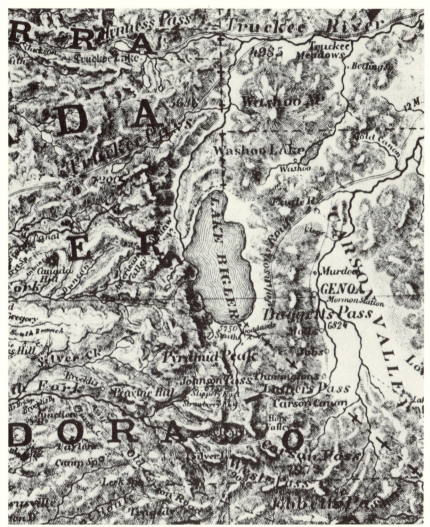

Courtesy, The Bancroft Library

From George H. Goddard's map of 1857.
"Lake Bigler" is correctly located.

The following newspaper articles chronicle a campaign to rename Lake Bigler.

"Sierra Lake, would be so musical and appropriate a name for that basin of silver water on the Sierra summits, known as Lake Bigler. . . . A place so picturesque, so destined to become the greatest resort for health, novelty and enjoyment in the known world, ought not to bear the name of an individual; or if so, it should not take a name which carries one into the Kitchen Cabinet of the traitor James Buchanan, or into that species of Copperheadism which breathes nothing but condemnation for the glorious defenders of our Government, and covert sympathy with treason. . . . [Sierra Lake would be very well, or the Indian name of the lake, Teho.—Eds. Union.]" (*Sacramento Daily Union*, May 28, 1863.)

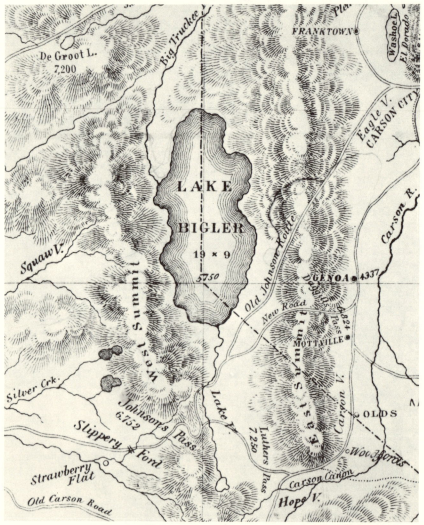

De Groot's map of 1860 indicated the roads. The controversy over Lake Tahoe's name had not yet begun.

"Tahoe Lake.—A correspondent of the *Bulletin*, writing from the vicinity of a beautiful sheet of water once known as Lake Bigler, has the following:

"Lake Bigler is a magnificent sheet of water. It has an area of 300 square miles. It has been sounded to the depth of 2,400 feet without finding bottom. It is 6,000 feet above the level of the ocean. . . . Finer drinking water I have never tasted—cool, pure as water can be, invigorating, it seems to infuse new life into the system. . . . Being but half a day's ride from Virginia, it is destined to become the favorite resort of the denizens of that fast growing city. In fact, I believe as it becomes more and more known it will become the great resort of Californians." (*Sacramento Daily Union*, May 29, 1863.)

"What's In a Name?—A correspondent of the Union suggests that it would be sensible to change the name of Lake Bigler to Sierra Lake. We think not, for there is already a Sierra Lake near the Downieville Buttes. Perhaps it might be more euphonious to Italianize the present name to *Lago Beergler*, which would stand always as a punning allusion to the bibulous habits which were reputed to characterize 'Honest John' when he was Governor of the State.—*Marysville Appeal*.

"As we have before intimated, the Indian name, Tahoe, will do. We are opposed to the appellations both of Lake Bigler and *Lago Beergler*, as unpleasantly suggestive at this time. If a lake of beer should be discovered, we might continue in the *Appeal's* amendment." (*Sacramento Daily Union*, May 30, 1863.)

"Tahoe.—It is proposed to drop the name of Bigler from the lake among the Sierras and adopt the Indian name of Tahoe. Good idea. Why the finest sheet of water in the mountains should be named after a fifth rate politician we have never been able to see. Let's call it Tahoe. Fine fishing in Tahoe. Who's going on a pleasant excursion this Summer to Tahoe? Poetical name; Indian name; proper name. Tahoe is suitable. Who don't say Tahoe?—*Nevada Transcript*." (*Sacramento Daily Union*, June 1, 1863.)

"Whether the change in name from Bigler to Tahoe has caused it to shrink within its limits, is a question for politicians and not for philosophers." (*Sacramento Daily Union*, August 13, 1863.)

"Lake Tahoe.—The Reese River *Reveille* suggests a change in the name of Lake Tahoe. . . . The discoverer of the lake, and the first to give it a place upon the map of the world, was Amande [Aimé] Bonpland a great traveler. . . . The name of Bonpland is given to the lake that is now Bigler or Tahoe. . . . Let the name Bonpland remain on the maps of France. We can get along with that of Tahoe, of Indian origin. It would hardly be consistent with the fitness of things of the present time for residents on the Pacific coast to give up an Indian name for that of a Frenchman." (*Sacramento Daily Union*, June 21, 1864. The *Daily Union's* patriotic sentiment was unnecessary, since Bonpland most certainly was not the discoverer of Lake Tahoe.)

Nellie Sanchez gave San Francisco Unitarian minister Thomas Starr King credit for publicizing the Washoe Indian name in his sermon "Living Waters from Lake Tahoe," which he wrote after a visit to the lake in 1863. Portions of the sermon are reprinted in *Lake of the Sky.* (Sanchez, 309–10; James, *Lake*, 366–72.)

During 1862 and 1863 the name "Lake Tahoe" came into general use. Dr. Henry De Groot's *A Tracing of a Map of Nevada & Eastern California*, and Bancroft's *Map of the Pacific States*, both published in 1863, used the names "Bigler" and "Tehoe," but thereafter Bigler's name disappeared from the maps. De Groot wrote that since this was the time of the confederate rebellion, Governor Bigler was being denounced as a "'copperhead' and secessionist, and therefore unworthy of the honor to dedicate his name to so great a feature of natural scenery, and he [Thomas Starr King] appealed himself authority to christen it Lake Tahoe." (Sioli, 78. This is incorrect. King promoted the name "Tahoe," but he himself did not name the lake.)

Opposition to the Indian name or change of the Bigler name was fermenting. On January 5, 1869 the *Stockton Daily Gazette* reprinted a *Sonora Union Democrat* story suggesting that an Indian named Tahoe led a band of savages who murdered Missourian George T. Rothrock, his wife, and their two children on the Truckee River in 1845 or 1847. "While, as a general thing, we like Indian names for lakes, rivers and mountains, we must say 'Tahoe' is not our style of aborigine. And while ordinarily opposed to using nature's most beautiful works for perpetuating the names of private individuals, we are decidedly in favor of respecting the action of the brave old pioneers, who gave to this magnificent lake the honored name of one of their own number, who has since endeared himself to a host of friends by his private worth and made his mark in the history of the State by long, faithful and distinguished public services."

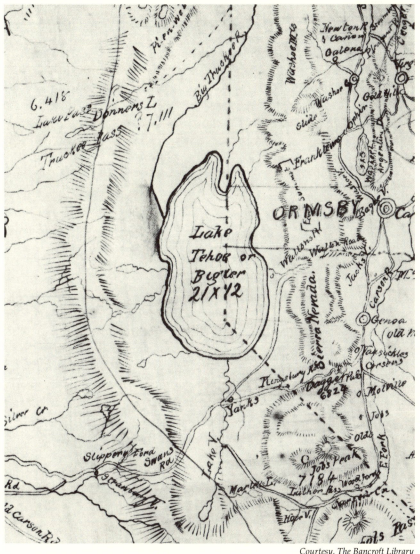

From De Groot's map of 1863. The name is now in transition, but Tahoe is spelled "Tehoe."

On February 10, 1870 the California Legislature passed an act to legalize the name "Lake Bigler." (*Statutes*, 1869–70, 64.) During the discussion, Mr. King from the Placer and Nevada [counties] delegations presented "Assembly Bill No. 226—An Act to legalize the name of Lake Bigler," which was "accompanied with a lengthy preamble reciting the fact that the lake was first named by a party of discovery from 'Hangtown,' now Placerville, of which the Governor was a member, and that in consequence of a conservative, though loyal letter, written by Governor Bigler in 1863, to the Democrats of Yuba county, his political opponents gave it the name of Tahoe. . . .

"The lake was named after Governor Bigler, not because he was a political leader, though he afterward became such, but because he succored emigrant parties, and did great good at personal sacrifice, sending rescue trains up into the snowy Sierra when his fellow men were perishing there utterly at the mercy of the elements.

"It was thought the beautiful lake deserved a beautiful name; that he [Mr. Doss] had heard a somewhat different story—to the effect that Tahoe was first suggested by a man named Dean, who kept a hotel at the upper end of the lake, and who gave it as his reason why the change should be made, that 'he did not want that lake to be named after the d—d rebel.' That was the language, precisely." The bill was read again and passed. In the same issue the following comments were made: "The question now arises whether the name of the entire sheet of water is to be changed or only part of it. The eastern boundary of this State, on the one hundred and twentieth meridian of west longitude, runs directly through the lake and almost in the center. The State of Nevada owns one-half of it, and are determined to call their portion Tahoe. Whatever our Legislature may conclude to do in this christening business, we think the latter name will prevail." (*Sacramento Daily Union*, February 2, 1870.)

A citizen from Nevada named Laguna wrote that the name should be "'Lake Union,' for the line which divides the two great States of California and Nevada and passes nearly through the center of the lake and divides it longitudinally, and a mutual name should be agreed upon by both States." (*Sacramento Daily Union*, February 3, 1870.)

"Lake Tahoe Again.—The Virginia *Enterprise* of February 3d has the annexed in this connection:

"An old resident of Nevada, whose name will be recognized by many, sends us the following communication in relation to the original meaning of the name of Lake Tahoe. The 'inclosure' referred to in the first paragraph is a scrap cut from the San Joaquin *Republican*, asserting that the word 'Tahoe' has a vulgar signification, and was at one time— and possibly may be yet—borne by a Washoe Indian noted for his rascality. It is further asserted (and the *State Capital Reporter*, Bigler's paper, indorses the story) that the name was selected by Bayard Taylor. Now, read what our correspondent says—what is said by the man who selected the name:

"GENOA, February 1, 1970.

"Dear Sir: A friend sends me the inclosed all the way from San Diego. He well knows that it is a Democratic fiction, and that Bayard Taylor had as little to do with originating the name of Tahoe as the editor of the *Republican*. The facts in regard to changing the name of the lake are these: Judge Dean, who is now in the Department of Agriculture, Washington, W. Van Wagner and myself—all strong Union men—were the original proprietors of the old Lake House, situated at the south end of the lake; and when Bigler was venting his Democratic spleen and rebellious ideas; when we found him acting with the disunion party of California, and using his best efforts to carry that State out of the Union, we determined to change the name of the lake and wipe out the name of Bigler, if possible. A variety of names were suggested and discussed, but I insisted on an Indian title. I wanted the name of Washoe retained for this State instead of Nevada, believing it more appropriate, particularly as it perpetuates the title of a tribe of men that must soon pass away and be forgotten. It has an historical significance that, to my mind, is eminently appropriate—far more so than the hackneyed Spanish name of Nevada. Consequently, we sounded every Indian we met for the Indian name of the lake. One of them, more intelligent than the rest, replied, 'Taa–oo'—meaning 'big water.' The next day quite a number of the Washoe tribe came to our house, and among them Captain Jim, who spoke English very freely, and we then settled the question of pronunciation. 'Tah–oo,' with the accent strong on the first syllable, is the correct Indian pronunciation, and means, as said before, 'big water.' A communication addressed to the *Sacramento Union*, proposing the change, was written by S. Dean, and published in that paper. Other papers adopted the new title and a long and bitter controversy ensued. Bayard Taylor selected it in his 'Views Afoot,' and changed the orthography to Tahoe. WE got a Post Office established at our house (I being the first Postmaster) under the title of Tahoe. A small town sprang up at the outlet, and we persuaded them to call it Tahoe City—which they did, and which name it still bears. I incline to the opinion that the Biglerites will find it exceedingly difficult to wash out the name.

"I do not write this for publication, but simply to inform you of the facts of the case. You, of course, are welcome to make any use of them that you desire.

"Respectfully yours, R. G. Dean." (*Sacramento Daily Union*, February 5, 1870.)

Not until 1945 did the California Legislature make the name "Lake Tahoe" the official name. (*Statutes*, 1945, 2777.)

Courtesy, The Bancroft Library

Bancroft's *Map of the Pacific States*, 1863, still had both names and the "Tehoe" spelling. Thereafter, Bigler's name was no longer used.

The origin of the name Tahoe is as yet uncertain. Frémont recorded only two Washoe Indian words: *"Tah-ve*, a word signifying snow," and "Mélo—a word signifying friend." (Frémont, *Expedition*, 228.) Captain J. H. Simpson obtained the following Washoe words from Major Frederick Dodge, Indian Agent in 1859: "Sea" and "Lake" are *Ta-hou*; "River" is *Wa-tah*; "Fish" is *Ou-wa-chee*. (Simpson, *California*, 470.) Dr. Henry De Groot claimed to have obtained the name Tahoe from Washoes during his exploration in 1859. Jim, Captain of the Washoe tribe of Indians, stated in 1863: "The meaning of it [Tahoe] is 'big–water.'" (*Sacramento Daily Union*, February 2, 1870.) Charles Crocker wrote: "I have ascertained that the meaning of the word 'Tahoe' is 'Big Water.' It is a Washoe Indian word, and I am unable to say from what it is derived, but that is its meaning." (Crocker.) "The Washo lived around the lake and referred to it as *Da ow a ga*, which means 'edge of the lake.' White people who mispronounced *Da ow* as 'Tahoe' gave the lake its English name." (Nevers, 5.)

"It is a pity that the original pronunciation of our grandest inland water [has] not . . . been preserved, the Washoe Indians articulating the word into three syllables—thus, Tah-ho-ee, instead of two, as is now the custom. It might be well for the newspapers of the State to look after and endeavor to rectify this error, as the primitive sound is much the more euphoneous, besides being more in accordance with the analogy of the Washoe dialect." (*San Francisco Mining and Scientific Press*, August 13, 1887.)

"Tahoe" as She is Spoke.

They were discussing the beauties of our grand mountain lake.

First tourist—I think that Lake Taw–who is simply magnificent.

Second tourist—Tay-o's sunsets are especially gorgeous.

Third tourist—And the water; I never saw such a beautiful shade of blue as in Lake T'-hoo.

Fourth tourist—They say that the body of a person drowned in Lake Tay-how never rises.

Fifth tourist—I never ate finer trout than are caught in Lake Taw-o.

Sixth tourist—I'm going to fetch my aunt and mother-in-law up to *Tay*-ho next summer.

Seventh tourist—I declare I mustn't miss going to Ta-ho [short "a"] to-morrow.

Just then the reporter remarked that *Tah*-hoe was attracting larger crowds of pleasure-seekers every year.—*Truckee Republican*." (*Sacramento Daily Record Union*, August 24, 1886.)

There may have been earlier discoveries than Frémont's, the origin of the name "Tahoe" may never be fully clarified, yet Tahoe was, without a doubt, one of the most beautiful natural areas on the North American continent that explorers had yet discovered.

"We cannot describe Lake Tahoe, because this paper is not canvas; and if it were, there are no colors rich and pure enough to portray that marvelous sheet of liquid sapphire—these purple peaks, the unspeakable air (which never puts off its transparency but to put on the exquisite pale blue of distance); nor is there any art by which to express the hush and stillness, unbroken but by rippling water and the crooning pines, and above all, that ineffable sense of being lifted up in the eyries of the clouds, and where the world's tumults cannot come." (*Sacramento Daily Union*, July 27, 1863.)

Tahoe City   California: Placer
Tahoe City

A Washoe Indian camp site, called *daubayOdu'E'*, meaning "running over," was located on a small hill, and was destroyed by highway construction. "The Washo fished and collected grasshoppers which were roasted over hot coals. About a mile north of here on the lake shore was a cave where the Washo collected swallows' eggs. The camp site which was near this cave is now under water." (Freed, *Washo*, 81.)

"Tahoe City.—The Dutch Flat *Enquirer* wrote: The miners have laid out a town at the mouth of Lake Tahoe, which they have christened Tahoe City, where, we understand, quite a number of persons intend remaining the Winter. Those who have any idea of the extent of the mines in the neighborhood of Squaw Valley appear very sanguine as to their richness." (*Sacramento Daily Union*, November, 4, 1863.)

James wrote that the town was founded in 1864 at the closing of the Squaw Valley mining operations. "Practically all its inhabitants were from the deserted town of Knoxville." (James, *Lake*, 199.) "By 1871 the little town of Tahoe City had a store, a blacksmith shop, a dairy, and several residences." (*Carson City Daily State Register*, July 11, 1871.) The post office was established on June 21, 1871. (Salley, 218.) Hoffmann's 1873 map showed "Tahoe City."

"SNOW-BOUND AT LAKE TAHOE. . . . After waiting two days for the Tahoe road to be opened, we were comfortably packed into a beautiful sleigh drawn by strong horses, able to take our party safely through to the Lake. Being the first ladies who have ever conceived the wild idea of expressly viewing this gem of the Sierras in its Winter loveliness, starting off well-prepared for any terrible storm, there was a cheer and a *'Bon voyage!'* as we dashed up the hill to the music of the jingling bells. . . .

Courtesy, The Bancroft Library

Tahoe City, two years after it was founded. From a sketch by Vischer.

Courtesy, California Historical Society, San Francisco

Grand Central Hotel, Tahoe City. Photo by R. E. Wood, 1880s.

"How shall I ever describe the wondrously beautiful scenery on the way? The whole land wore a pure, clean white carpet, over which a spangling frost had showered, dazzling by the brilliancy of its diamond sparkle as far as the eye could reach. . . .

". . . The first view of the Lake broke upon our sight, but the storm - continuing almost blinded us, while Tahoe dashed and moaned in breakers on the beach like a small ocean. Arriving at the Tahoe House we were soon cosily settled and kindly attended to, and were really astonished to find everything so enjoyably arranged about us. Comfortable rooms and delicious food, including fresh trout, made it a welcome retreat, aside from its being the point embracing the most magnificent and expansive view of the lake.

"'I fear,' said King, the landlord, the next morning, 'that you are snow-bound, the storm continuing, and the snow up to this time having fallen to an additional depth of three feet since your arrival. . . .'" (*Sacramento Daily Union*, February 5, 1869.)

"The fish hatchery at Tahoe [City], constructed by Commodore Todman, is about to commence active operations. Spawn will be taken next week and it is expected that a million young fish will be put into the lake this season. Capt. Frasier has charge of the work." (*Truckee Republican*, May 4, 1887.)

Tahoe Mountain   California: El Dorado
Emerald Bay

The mountain is about two miles south of Lake Tahoe and just east of Fallen Leaf Lake. It appears that George H. Goddard made the sketch reproduced on the front cover of this book from the summit of Tahoe Mountain.

Tahoe National Forest   California: Placer
Kings Beach

Lake Tahoe Forest Reserve was created by proclamation of President William McKinley on April 13, 1899, and Yuba Forest Reserve was created by proclamation of President Theodore Roosevelt on November 11, 1905. On September 17, 1906 President Roosevelt consolidated the two units into the Tahoe National Forest. (Ayers, 6.)

Tahoe Pines   California: Placer
Homewood

The location was known earlier only as "Idlewild," which was the name of the summer home of the Edwin B. Crocker family. In 1905

Fredrick C. Kohl of San Francisco bought the Crocker home. Kohl sold it to Herbert Fleischhacker of San Francisco in 1926, who sold it to Evert Mills, who subdivided the property. Later the A. R. Bradleys owned the home "Idlewild." (Scott, 63–68.) Tahoe Pines post office was established March 21, 1912. (Salley, 218. See **Idlewild**.)

Tahoe State Park   California: Placer
Tahoe City

The state of California acquired thirteen acres near Tahoe City in 1899 for $1,000, and designated the area as a campground in 1919. The name "Tahoe State Park" was applied in 1927 when the State Park Commission acquired the property. This was also the year in which the California state park movement organized and supported legislation that created the State Parks Commission. (Strong, 85–86.)

Tahoe Valley   California: El Dorado
South Lake Tahoe

In the late 1870s some 280 acres of meadowland belonged to Thomas Benton Rowland, who operated a hotel—"Rowland's," in the Al Tahoe area—and a dairy in the meadowlands. The name Tahoe Valley now refers to an area within the city of South Lake Tahoe near the "Y." (Scott, 209. See **Al Tahoe**.) "Tahoe Valley" appeared on the USGS *South Lake Tahoe* quad, 1955. A post office opened here on June 12, 1940. (Salley, 218.)

Tahoe Vista   California: Placer
Kings Beach

A Washoe and Paiute Indian trail led from Martis Valley—whose Indian name was *Timilick*—east over the divide to the lake in the Tahoe Vista area. From 1849 to 1852 the trail was a branch of the Emigrant Trail. D. H. Wright built the Pine Grove Station in 1865, and in 1910 Morris Brooks and Charles W. Paine (Tahoe Development Co.) built the Tahoe Vista Hotel. (Scott, 335–36.) A post office was established on July 18, 1911. (Salley, 218. See **Martis**.)

Tahoma   California: Placer
Homewood

Joseph Bishop, San Francisco chimney sweep and brother-in-law of lumberman Augustus Colwell, named the property he acquired from Colwell, "Tahoma," which—according to Bishop—meant "place away from home that would mean home to his guests." Bishop built and

operated the Tahoma Resort hotel and cottages from 1916 to 1920.
(Scott, 95.) Salley called Tahoma a "'synthetic name,' a take-off from
Tahoe." A post office was established September 1, 1946. (Salley, 218.)

Talking Mountain   California: El Dorado
Echo Lake

Echoes are said to resound from this mountain. The name appeared
on the 1955 *Fallen Leaf* 15-minute quad and the Forest Service 1945
map.

Courtesy, California State Library

Tallac House.

Tallac, Mount; Tallac: Creek, Lake   California: El Dorado
Emerald Bay

The mountain appeared as "Crystal Peak" on Goddard's map, *Sierra region south of Lake Tahoe*, on Hoffmann's map of 1873, and on the
1874 von Leicht-Hoffmann map. "Mount Tahlac," its original name,
"in the Indian vernacular of this section, means 'Great Mountain.'"
(*Carson City Appeal*, August 12, 1875.) It would seem that "Tahlac" was
a Washoe Indian common noun rather than a proper name. Captain

J. H. Simpson's report included the Washoe word for "mountain"—*Ta-lah-act*. (Simpson, *California*, 470.) "Tallac Peak" and "Tallac House" are on the Wheeler map of 1881.

E. J. Baldwin bought 1,000 acres from Ephraim "Yank" Clement in 1878, and in 1879 built the famed first-class hotel, Tallac House. (James, *Lake*, 208. See **Baldwin Beach**.) "Tallac House is the hotel of the Lake— is strictly first-class, can entertain 250 people. Music and other refined enjoyments are liberally provided, supplemented by boating, fishing, hunting, riding, driving and mountain climbing that should satisfy the most exacting. A specially well-stocked livery establishment is accessory." (*Sierra Highlands*.) The resort operated until the early 1920s. (Greuner, 45.)

Alfred R. Conkling wrote: "The finest scenery is found in the southwestern corner of Lake Tahoe, near Tallac Peak. There is no part of the United States that surpasses this region in scenery. In my extensive travels on the continent of Europe I have seen but one lake more picturesque than Tahoe, viz, the Lake of Luzerne, in Switzerland." (Wheeler, *Report*, 1295.)

Tamarack Lake   California: El Dorado
Echo Lake

Tamarack incorrectly refers to the true Tamarack pine (*Larix* or Eastern Larch), which does not grow in California. Most likely the name referred to the lodgepole pine (*Pinus murrayana*); the confusion originates from its other name, tamrac. (Storer, 149.) It was a common mistake. Joseph LeConte wrote on August 19, 1870: "On we went, at a good round pace, and camped at 7 P.M. in a fine grove of tamaracks, on the very borders of the lake." (LeConte, *Ramblings*, 96.) And James referred to tamarack in *Lake of the Sky*. (James, *Lake*, 223.) The *Glen Alpine Lake Tahoe Forest Reserve California* pamphlet printed in 1906 used the name "Tamarack Lake."

Taylor Creek   California: El Dorado
Emerald Bay

The creek probably is named for Elijah W. Taylor, who patented 160 acres near the creek on December 18, 1864. "[Fallen Leaf Lake's] only outlet is a small mountain stream, which meanders for a distance of about 3 miles, and then empties into Lake Tahoe. The land between the two lakes is quite level, and as a good trail leads over it, it is a pleasant walk from one to the other." (*San Francisco Daily Evening Bulletin*, August 31, 1863.) Washoe Indians are known to have camped at

Taylor Creek. Freed mentioned it as a bedrock mortar site. (Freed, *Washo*, 82.) C. F. McGlashan described the Indians fishing at Taylor Creek. (*Sacramento Daily Record Union*, May 29, 1875.) The Washoe Indians together with the US Forest Service have made plans to build a Washoe Cultural Center on Taylor Creek. "Research by the Nevada Archaeological Survey indicates that the [Taylor Creek] project site is one of the most significant Washoe campsites within the Tahoe Basin." (*Washoe*, i.)

Third Creek   Nevada: Washoe
Marlette Lake
Mt. Rose
Named in succession with First and Second creeks, all of which flow into Crystal Bay. (See **First Creek**.)

Thompson Peak   California: Alpine
Freel Peak
The peak is named for John Albert "Snowshoe" Thompson (1827–1876), a native of Norway. The Thompson family came to this country in 1837 and settled in Illinois until 1838, Missouri in 1839, Iowa in 1841, and back to Illinois in 1845. Young Thompson came overland to Placerville in 1851, where he worked as a miner for the Coon Hollow and Kelsey Diggings. Later he moved to Putah Creek, where he farmed from 1854 to 1855. (*Virginia City Daily Territorial Enterprise*, February 13, 1876.)

It was here that he heard about the difficulty of carrying the mail across the Sierra in winter. Recalling his early days in Norway, he fashioned ten-foot-long skis from California oak, and went to the Sierra. Thompson reported that he made the second trip of the winter of 1856–57 "on his Norwegian snow shoes, seven and a half feet long, over snow which, at some points, he was unable to fathom." (*Sacramento Daily Union*, January 10, 1857.)

"Late from Carson Valley. Mr. A. J. Thompson, the Carson Valley Expressman, called upon us yesterday, having made his first trip this year from the Valley. The journey was as usual, in winter, performed on foot. He left Carson Valley on Thursday, Dec. 4th, and reached Placerville on Monday night, Dec. 8th. On Thursday night, Mr. Thompson stopped at the cabin of 'Uncle Billy Rodgers,' in Hope Valley. . . .

"In Carson Valley, when Mr. Thompson left, there was about four inches of snow; and on the summit of the Sierras, for a distance of about thirty miles, there was a depth of three feet. . . .

"Mr. Thompson says that if by next season something is not done by Sacramento and Placerville towards the opening of the road by the way of Johnson's cut-off, the travel will all go by the way of Murphy's. Mr. Thompson came by the old Carson road.

"Provisions were not very abundant in the Valley. Flour was selling for 15 cents per lb.; barley, 4 cents; beef, 15 to 16 cents." (*Sacramento Daily Union*, December 10, 1856.)

In traversing the wilderness, Thompson more than once had the occasion to rescue people caught in snowstorms in the high mountainous terrain between Placerville and Genoa. "About Christmas, in the year 1856, he saved the life of James Sisson, who had laid in an old deserted cabin in Lake Valley twelve days with his feet frozen. . . . When found by 'Snow-shoe Thompson'. . . his legs were purple to the knees. He was confident that mortification had set in and knew that if his legs were not amputated he must soon die. . . . Thompson went to Genoa and there raised a party of six men. . . . They arrived at the cabin in the evening and that night built a hand-sled on which to carry the frozen man to Carson Valley. . . . The first night they got no farther than Hope Valley, where they camped. The next day they arrived at Genoa. The doctors found that it would be necessary to amputate both of Sisson's feet. Before the operation could be performed Thompson had to make a trip to Sacramento for chloroform. Sisson was in the Atlantic States when last heard from." (*Virginia City Daily Territorial Enterprise*, February 13, 1876.)

"Mr. Thompson has crossed the Sierra Nevadas *thirty-one* times during the winter months, generally on snow-shoes. . . . He never carries a blanket or other covering, save a common suit of winter clothes. When night overtakes him, he kindles a fire by some dry stump or tree-top, and lies down by its side. These extra-ordinary exposures never produce colds; but as soon as he reaches the settlements, and after breathing [the] atmosphere of confined rooms, he at once becomes subject to these annoyances. The greatest difficulty in his travels, is from the sun's reflection from the crystallized snows of the untimbered mountain summits. So intense is this light that it sometimes causes total blindness, and crisps and parches the skin of the face like the heat from a furnace." (*Sacramento Daily Union*, April 23, 1857.)

Thompson made the eastward journey in three days and the return in two days. "The weight of the bags he carried was generally from sixty to eighty pounds, but one winter, when he carried the overland mail for Chorpenning, his load often weighed over one hundred pounds." (*Virginia City Daily Territorial Enterprise*, February 13, 1876.)

Courtesy, Nevada Historical Society

"Snowshoe" Thompson.

Thompson had no fear of the wilderness, the deep snow, or the wildlife. "Not a house was found in all the distance [he traveled]. Between the two points all was a howling wilderness. It was a Siberia of snow." (Ibid.) He never carried blankets and never wore an overcoat.

"I was never frightened but once during all my travels in the mountains; that was in the winter of 1857. I was crossing Hope Valley, when I came to a place where six great wolves—big timber wolves—were at work digging up the carcass of some animal. They looked to have hair on them a foot long. They were great, gaunt, shaggy fellows. My course lay near them. I knew I must show a bold front. I might run away from a bear, but these were customers of a different kind. There was nothing of them but bones, sinews and hair, and they could skim over the snow like birds.

"As I approached they left the carcass and came out in single file a distance of about twenty-five yards toward my line of march. The leader of the pack then wheeled about and sat down on his haunches. When the next came up he did the same and so on till all were seated in a line. They acted just like trained soldiers. I pledge you my word I thought the devil was in them. There they sat, every nose turned toward me as I approached. Just when I was opposite them and but about twenty-five yards away the leader threw back his head and began a howl. All the rest of the pack did the same. . . . A more horrible sound I never heard. I thought it meant my death. The awful yell rang out across the silent valley and was echoed by the hills—was re-echoed far away among the mountains. I felt my hair raise on my head, but I put on a bold front. I passed by them as a general passes in front of the soldiers he is reviewing. I did not alter my gait, nor did I turn an inch to the right or left. I kept my course as though the wolves had not been there. They uttered but their first awful howl. When they saw that that did not make me run they feared to come after me; so they let me pass, and when I was far away I saw them going back to the carcass. (Ibid.)

Thompson was known as an authority and a keen spokesman on the best mountain routes. California state surveyor Sherman Day wrote: "Of all the men who have published reports, comparing the Big Trees route with the Placerville route, Mr. John A. Thompson, the Expressman, seems to be the only man who is familiar with both routes. I take his statement with implicit reliance, and have as full confidence that the Big Trees route is the best for the Southern mining counties, as I have that the Placerville route is the best for the heart of the State."(*Sacramento Daily Union*, May 19, 1857.)

"Thompson has two sleighs and two teams of mules, with which he travels the road daily. His headquarters are in Lake Valley, and his plan is to start one team west and the other east. That traveling west comes over the summit and as far as Silver creek, where it strikes the new road down the American river. To that point wagons manage to haul goods, and there Thompson takes them on his sleigh and runs them over to Lake Valley. The next morning the team for the mouth of Carson Cañon is harnessed to the sleigh, upon which the goods are loaded; the other starts back to Silver creek for another load. The sleigh for the mouth of Carson Cañon delivers its freight at Woodford's, which is twelve miles from Lake Valley, and from there it is hauled to Genoa, eleven miles further, in a wagon. It is about thirteen miles from Lake Valley to Silver creek, which makes the distance traveled on snow twenty-five miles. The sub-Indian Agent for the Indians on the east side of the Sierra Nevada, Frederick Dodge, who came over from Carson in the stage day before yesterday, declares that portion traveled in sleighs to be really a pleasure trip." (*Sacramento Daily Union*, January 12, 1859.)

In addition to providing transport over the snowy mountains, Thompson found time to write articles for the *Sacramento Daily Union*, and compete in ski racing. Frank Stewart, a carpenter and ski-maker, beat Snowshoe Thompson in a ski race in Plumas County and won five hundred dollars in gold dust. Stewart's skis were much lighter than Thompson's, and he also used a ski wax called "dope," which he had invented. (*Sacramento Daily Union*, April 7, 1869.)

"'I have seen Thompson,' said the Buoy, 'jump a cut sixty feet wide, and go as if it were not there. Talk about your acrobats and flying trapeze! They had a snowshoe race over at Silver two years ago between Thompson and five or six Norwegians. There was a gap in the fence they had to go through near the end of the track, and the Norway fellows crowded Thompson out, but he jumped the fence and beat them in—distance, half a mile—time, eleven seconds and a quarter.'

"I took out a note book and commenced to make some figures.

"'What are you figuring at,' said the Buoy, in his ominous bass.

"'I was trying to calculate how long it would take a stone to fall half a mile,' I replied meekly.

"'What has that to do with it, young vulgar fractions,' he retorted, deeper and fiercer than ever. 'Suppose you calculate how long it would take lightning to do it. I tell you,' in his shrillest treble, 'Thompson on snow-shoes is lightning!'" ("A Holiday Excursion With H. C. Watson," *Sacramento Daily Union*, January 1, 1873.)

Thompson is buried in Genoa, Nevada.

The Gibbes map of 1866 has the words 'Thompsons Pk' applied southwest of the wagon road over Luther Pass, apparently on what is now named "Waterhouse Peak." "The exact position of the peak could not be determined because of the lack of sufficient topographic detail." (USGS, 1958. See **Waterhouse Peak**.)

Thunder Cliff California: Placer
Tahoe City

The origin is unknown, but it may be conjectured that storms coming from the north often seem to produce thunder from these cliffs.

Toiyabe National Forest Nevada and California
Kings Beach
Martis Peak
South Lake Tahoe

Kroeber recorded two variants of the Shoshone word for "mountain:" *toyap* and *toyavi*. (Kroeber, *Shoshonean*, 95.) The Nevada forest reserve was named for the Toiyabe Mountains, the name of which dates from 1867. (Ayers, 9.) In 1908 the US Board on Geographic Names decided on the spelling "Toyabe," but later changed its decision to agree with local usage. In 1946 a portion of Mono National Forest was added to Toiyabe National Forest. The forest was enlarged again by an act passed on June 16, 1950. (USGS, 1968.)

Triangle Lake California: El Dorado
Echo Lake

Named for its shape. The name appeared on the *Fallen Leaf* 15-minute quad, 1955, and the Forest Service map of 1945. According to the USFS pamphlet *Trails of the Lake Tahoe Basin*, the Triangle Lake Trail offers a magnificent view of Fallen Leaf Lake and the Glen Alpine area.

Trout Creek California: El Dorado
Freel Peak
South Lake Tahoe

The Washoe Indian name for Trout Creek is *mathOcahuwO'tha*. The word *mathOcauwa* means "white fish" (*Coregonus williamsoni Girard*), and *wO'tha* means "river."

"This was an important fall camp on Trout Creek. The Washo camped here for white fish and late berries. Trout Creek was different from the other streams because here the people could live near their fish blinds. They did not have to camp together since there were no wild animals in the area at this time of year. This was the last camp on the lake. People prepared whitefish to take with them into the Pine Nut Mountains or into California, where they obtained acorns." (Freed, *Washo*, 78.) The names "Trout Creek, East Branch, West Branch" appeared on the Wheeler map of 1881.

Truckee River   California: Placer
Tahoe City

In January 1844 Frémont camped beside a river near Pyramid Lake. "An Indian brought in a large fish to trade. . . . [The] flavor was excellent—superior, in fact, to that of any fish I have ever known. . . .

"They made on the ground a drawing of the river, which they represented as issuing from another lake in the mountains three or four days distant, in a direction a little west of south; beyond which, they drew a mountain; and further still, two rivers; on one of which they told us that people like ourselves travelled.

". . . I tried unsuccessfully to prevail on some of them to guide us for a few days on the road, but they only looked at each other and laughed.

"This morning we continued our journey along this beautiful stream, which we naturally called the Salmon Trout river. (Frémont, *Expedition*, 218–19.)

In late September of 1844 the Elisha Stevens and Dr. Townsend party, originating from Council Bluffs, Iowa, was at the sink of the Humboldt River in what is now western Nevada. Their guide's knowledge of the route did not extend west of the Rockies, and they did not know what direction to take. "Finally an old Indian was found, called Truckee, with whom old man Greenwood talked by means of signs [and] diagrams drawn on the ground. From it was learned that fifty or sixty miles to the west there was a river that flowed easterly from the mountains, and that along this stream they [*sic*] were large trees and good grass. Acting on this information, Dr. Townsend, Captain Stevens, and Joseph Foster, taking Truckee as a guide, started out to explore this route, and after three days returned, reporting that they had found the river just as the Indian had described it." Two days later "they reached the river, which they named the Truckee in honor of the old Indian chief, who had piloted them to it." ("Trip of the Murphy Party," *San Jose Pioneer and Historical Review*, April 15, 1893.)

"Truckee River was named after an old Indian known as 'Truckee,' who acted as guide for a party of emigrants on their way to California in 1844. He guided them from where he met them, on the Humboldt near where Battle Mountain now is, to the one little river which now bears his name, given it by the party in honor of their guide, to whom they had already become much attached." (*San Francisco Daily Alta California*, May 10, 1875.)

An early trapper and guide, James P. Beckwourth, wrote that in April 1851 "We struck across this beautiful valley to the waters of the Yuba, from thence to the Truchy, which latter flowed in an easterly direction." (Farquhar, 94.)

The name "Truckey" appeared on T. H. Jefferson's *Map of the Emigrant Road*, 1849. (Wheat, vol. 3, Map 624.)

Princess Winnemucca, granddaughter of Chief Truckee, who was the chief of the entire Paiute nation, reported that Frémont named him Chief Truckee, and that he served as guide for Frémont. (Edwards, 98.) "He showed Nelson [Nelson's Mining Camp near Palmyra, Nevada] and his companions a small Bible presented to him by Colonel Fremont, and with Fremont's name inscribed on the fly leaf; also a copy of the St. Louis *Republican* and other papers. . . . [He] told them considerable about Fremont and other of the early explorers and emigrants with whom he was connected and acquainted. The Bible was buried with Captain Truckee." (Edwards. 99.) Captain Truckee "died near Como, Palmyra district, Lyon county, Nevada in 1860, and was decently buried by white men." (*San Francisco Daily Alta California*, May 10, 1875.)

Although Lake Tahoe is fed by thirty-seven streams, the Truckee River is the lake's only outlet. (*San Francisco Daily Alta California*, June 21, 1870.) In 1871 the outflow measured 800,000,000 gallons per day. (*San Francisco Daily Alta California*, February 28, 1871.) In 1888 it was reported to discharge 923,400,000 gallons in twenty-four hours. (*Truckee Republican*, May 2, 1888.) Just a week later the same newspaper reported: "Very little water is flowing out of Lake Tahoe and the gates of the dam at the outlet are all raised. The water of the lake is lower than ever before but there was a time before the advent of the whites when it was much lower than now. This fact is demonstrated in the following way: There is a large flat rock near the shore of the lake which is now above water, but which no white man can ever remember of having seen dry before. An inspection of the rock, however discloses in its surface several large round holes, evidently made by Indians in pounding acorns, and it is probable that years and years ago the Natives used to grind acorns and pine nuts on that rock which must have been above water. Thus the water in Tahoe must at some time in the past have been lower than now." (*Truckee Republican*, May 9, 1888.)

"In 1889 and 1890, under the direction of Maj. J[ohn] W[esley] Powell, director of the United States Geological Survey, systematic investigations were begun on the flow of the Truckee River and tributary streams, and reconnaissance of lakes considered feasible for storage reservoirs were made. . . . On January 11, 1902, the director of the Geological Survey . . . submitted to the Secretary of the Interior a report upon the utilization of Lake Tahoe as a reservoir of water for irrigation purposes, in which report it was held that by providing for control of six feet in depth on the lake, or an actual storage capacity of 750,000 acre-feet, an annual storage supply of 200,000 acre-feet could be depended upon for irrigation. . . . These plans . . . included the storing of water in Lake Tahoe, the construction of a canal from Truckee River, near Wadsworth, to the Carson River, a storage reservoir on Carson River, the necessary systems of distribution canals, and eventually other storage reservoirs in the Truckee and Carson River basins. . . . On March 14, 1903, the Secretary of the Interior approved the general project as recommended and authorized the preparation of plans and specifications for construction to be submitted to him for approval." (Davis, *Nevada*, 745–46.)

Truckee Marsh; Upper Truckee River   California: El Dorado
Echo Lake
South Lake Tahoe

Washoe Indians camped near the Upper Truckee and called the site *"ImgiwO'tha (Imgi,* cutthroat trout; . . . *wO'tha,* river). This camp was two hundred yards east of the Upper Truckee River and about one and one-fourth miles from the lake. As the name implies, it was important for trout fishing." (Freed, *Washo*, 78.)

George H. Goddard recorded the name "Upper Truckee" on his triangulation map and in his report in September 1855. "The lake, I suspect, is very deep in the center, as there is a well defined line of deep blue stretching out from a point on the eastern side, towards the mouth of the Upper Truckee. . . .

"At the mouth of the Upper Truckee, the stream is about fifty feet wide, with a depth of from two to six feet. It runs very slowly, and in some places has very deep pools. It, as well as the lake, is well stocked with trout. This was not, however, the season, and we did not procure any." (Goddard, *Report*, 113–14.)

"The little stream of the Upper Truckee, though but of yesterday, has yet carried down its sandy deposits through ages sufficient to form the five miles of valley flats, from the foot of the Johnson Pass to the present margin of the lake, and still the work progresses. The shallows at the mouth of the river are stretching across towards the first point on the eastern slope of the lake, and at the same time the water level of the lake is evidently subsiding." (Goddard, *Bigler*, 108.)

Also called "Little Truckee," "Lake Valley Creek," and "Lake Stream," the Upper Truckee is one of the many feeder creeks, streams, and rivers that flow into Lake Tahoe. The name "Truckee Marsh" was added to the map by the USGS in 1956.

Tucker Flat   California: El Dorado
Freel Peak

Gudde suggests that this location was named for a stockman and road builder named Tucker. (Gudde, 346.) "The Tucker Flat Trail offers beautiful views of the Hope Valley area east of Luther Pass." (USFS, *Trails of the Lake Tahoe Basin*.)

Tunnel Creek   Nevada: Washoe
Marlette Lake

Most likely named for its proximity to the tunnel that carries water through the mountain into Carson Valley.

Twin Crags   California: Placer
Tahoe City

Origin unknown. The name appeared on the 1944 Forest Service map and the *Tahoe* 15-minute quad, 1955. (See **Cracked Crag**.)

Twin Peaks   California: Placer
Homewood

"Ramsdale Buoy" named these the "Union Peaks" in 1866, because he thought they resembled two connected pyramids. ("A Cruise on a Mountain Sea," *Sacramento Daily Union*, August 4, 1866.) The name "Twin Peaks" appeared on the *Map of the Comstock Area*, circa 1875.

Velma Lakes: Lower, and Upper   California: El Dorado
Rockbound Valley

Only the Upper and Lower Velmas are in the Tahoe basin. In 1900 a Forest Service crew, at the request of Harry Oswald Comstock, manager of the Tallac House, named the Upper, Lower, and Middle Velma lakes for his baby daughter. (Eden.)

Courtesy, Jim Hildinger

Vikingsholm, 1971.

Vikingsholm   California: El Dorado
Emerald Bay

A Viking's castle, judged the finest example of Scandinavian architecture in North America, was designed by Lennart Palme, who was the husband of the niece of the owner, Mrs. Lora Josephine Moore Knight. Mrs. Knight bought the Emerald Bay property, including the island, from William Henry Armstrong in 1928 for $250,000.

Vikingsholm was completed in 1929. Mrs. Knight valued the natural beauty of the property, and directed the planning so as to avoid unnecessary destruction to the trees. (Scott, 131, 133.) She spent summers here until her death in 1945. Harvey West bought the property, and later donated half its value to the state. It became part of the State Park system in 1954. (Strong, 87. See **Emerald Bay** and **Fannette Island**.)

Von Schmidt Line 1873   California and Nevada
South Lake Tahoe

Named for Colonel Alexis Waldemar Von Schmidt (1821–1906), who in August 1872 undertook a state-financed survey of the boundary line between California and Nevada. Von Schmidt completed the survey in 1874 at the cost of $40,750. (Uzes, 90.)

Von Schmidt, a brilliant engineer, was born in Riga, Russia (Latvia). Nothing is known of his formal training, except that much of his technical knowledge was acquired from his father. He arrived in San Francisco in May 1849 after a journey from New York. For a time he was deputy surveyor for the US Surveyor General in San Francisco. (Reimer, ii.)

Not all of his ideas met with acceptance. One that did not was a plan to pipe Lake Tahoe water to San Francisco. "In reference to the rights of the two States in which Lake Tahoe is situated I think it would be well to consider their respective interests to the water in proportion to the respective portion of the lake in each State. One-third of the lake is east of the line dividing Nevada and California. The other two-thirds are in California as well as its outlet." (*Sacramento Daily Union*, October 15, 1866.) Some of his successes included developing and assembling the first pumping dredges on the Pacific Coast, designing and building the dry dock at Hunter's Point in San Francisco, and blowing up "Blossom Rock" in San Francisco Bay. Von Schmidt died in Alameda on May 26, 1906.

Ward: Creek, Peak   California: Placer
Homewood
Tahoe City

Named for Ward Rush, who on April 1, 1874 homesteaded 160 acres in sec. 12, T. 15 N., R. 16 E. "Ward's Cr" is shown on the Hoffmann map of 1873 and on the von Leicht-Hoffmann map of 1874. "Ward Peak" appeared on the Wheeler map of 1881. Both names are on the *Truckee* 30-minute map of 1889.

Washoe County   Nevada

Mt. Rose

The county, which was created on November 25, 1861, took its name from the Indian name, *Washiu,* meaning "person." (Swanton, 383.) "Traditionally, the people referred to the whole tribe with the phrase 'Wa She Shu.' The word 'Washo,' which originally meant 'one person,' is often used today to describe the whole tribe." (Nevers, 1.) The Washoe tribe inhabited Lake Tahoe and eastern Nevada. James F. Downs wrote that Lake Tahoe "is still the center of the Washo world. . . . Each creek flowing into the lake, each stand of trees or outcropping of rocks or lake in the high valleys is associated not only with the secular history of their people but with the sacred myth of the creation of the Washo world." (Downs, 1–2.)

"We have been all the winter in the seat of the Indian disturbances and have had plenty of false reports and exaggerations,—the unfortunate Indians are shot down like deer by the Americans . . . ." (Goddard letter to his brother, April 1851, CSL.)

"Nearly all the Indians of the vallies are now assembled at Lake Bigler, and are catching large quantities of fish. Their captain says: 'White man say Indian steal white man's cattle. I tell Indian not to steal cattle. Indian don't.'. . . The rumored trouble from the Indians of Carson, Wash-ho and Walker's Vallies, is entirely without foundation." (Report of Martin Smith, the first settler at Lake Tahoe, in the *Sacramento Daily Union,* May 26, 1856.)

By the following year relations had deteriorated. "I am also informed that one hundred Pyute Indians and twenty or thirty whites, under the command of Major Ormsby, were to start yesterday in pursuit of the Washoes and Little Valley Indians. . . . Major Ormsby sent an express, which arrived here this morning, for ammunition, &c., to be ready for an emergency. An Indian war is inevitable, as the frequent murders—saying nothing of robbery—by this tribe, calls for prompt action on the part of residents." (*Sacramento Daily Union,* October 5, 1857. See **Ormsby**.)

"The *Washoes,* according to Major Dodge, numbered in *1859* about nine hundred souls, and inhabited the country along the eastern slope of the Sierra Nevada, from Honey Lake, on the north, to the Clara, the west branch of Walker's River, a distance of one hundred and fifty miles. . . . In 1859 there was not one horse, pony, or mule in the nation. They are peaceable, but indolent. In the summer they wander around the shores of Lake Bigler, in the Sierra Nevada, principally subsisting on fish. In the winter they lie around in the arte mista (wild sage) of their different localities, subsisting on a little grass-seed." (Simpson, *Route*, 49.)

In 1861 Warren Wasson, US Indian Agent at the Carson Valley Agency, in reports to Governor Nye of Nevada Territory in July and August wrote: ". . . The Washoes number 550 . . . [and] have no property of any kind. . . . They have no schools. . . .

"As regards the Washoe tribes, I see no other resource than to aid them with provisions through the winter. . . . There is great justice in this request. The streams in which they formerly fished are now all spoiled for that purpose by the operations of the miners and the washing of the ores and metals. They are indeed most all diverted from their original courses, or dammed so frequently that the fish have disappeared from them. Lake Bigler, lying in the country of the Washoes, and from which they formerly obtained large quantities of the best kind of fish, is now taken possession of by the whites, and has become a watering place, to which large numbers from this Territory and California resort, and from which this poor tribe are virtually excluded. The hills and plains over which roamed plenty of game are now occupied by the whites, and the game has fled, like the Indians, from their presence." (Davis, v. 1, 35.)

> "Many a weary day went by,
> While wretched and worn he begged for bread;
> Tired of life, and longing to lie
> Peacefully down with the silent dead.
> Hunger and cold, and scorn and pain,
> Had wasted his form and seared his brain;
> At last on a bed of frozen ground
> In the 'Sierra Nevada' was the outcast found. . . ."
> (Dodge, in Davis, v. 1, 120.)

In 1925 Kroeber wrote: "Lake Tahoe is central to Washo territory, and was and is still resorted to in summer." (Kroeber, *Indians*, 570.) Washo is probably of the Hokan linguistic family. (Swanton, 383.)

Waterhouse Peak   California: El Dorado, Alpine
Freel Peak

The name was given in memory of Clark Waterhouse, who had been in charge of the Angora Lookout, and died in World War I. (Gudde, 359. See **Angora**.) USGS files cited problems identifying Waterhouse and Thompson peaks. (See **Thompson Peak**.)

Looking south along the west side of Lake Tahoe, near the
William Kent Campground and the site of Tahoe Tavern, about 1915.

Watson: Creek, Lake   California: Placer
Tahoe City

The lake and the creek were named for Robert Montgomery Watson, who came to Lake Tahoe in 1875. He purchased the hotel Tahoe House from William Pomin in 1888; Pomin had built the hotel in 1868. (*Truckee Republican*, April 18, 1888.) No better statement can be found to describe Bob Watson than the dedication written by George Wharton James in *Lake of the Sky*: "To Robert M. Watson (To his friends 'Bob') Fearless Explorer, Expert Mountaineer, Peerless Guide, Truthful Fisherman, Humane Hunter, Delightful Raconteur, True-Hearted Gentleman, Generous Communicator of a large and varied knowledge, Brother to Man and Beast and Devoted Friend." (James, *Lake*, vii.)

White Hill   Nevada: Douglas
Glenbrook

Origin unknown. The hill is half a mile southeast of Spooner Junction.

William Kent Station and **Campground**   California: Placer
Tahoe City

In the summer of 1903 William Kent and his family brought his ailing mother up to Lake Tahoe, and her health improved. The family purchased beach front property, and engaged an architect. "A simple commodious house was built," containing two large dorm-like room upstairs and five bedrooms downstairs. (Kent, 102.) In 1910 Kent was elected to Congress from Marin County, and served three terms. As a reform-minded congressman he wrote the bill that created the National Park Service in 1916. At home he supported the Save-the-Redwoods League and gave land for Muir Woods, which became a National Monument in 1908, and for the creation of Mount Tamalpais State Park, which was enacted July 29, 1937. (Teather, 38–39, 46; Schrepher, 12, 72.) In 1924 "Kent deeded 23 acres of beautiful forest land, with a lake frontage of nearly two hundred feet, to the United States. It was designated U.S. Public Camp Grounds. In 1949, at the request of the Forest Service, the name was changed to William Kent Public Camp Ground." (Kent, 363.)

"To give further fire protection a gasoline launch—the *Ranger*—twenty-six feet long and with a carrying capacity of fifteen men, and a speed of about nine miles an hour, was placed on Lake Tahoe in 1910, at the Kent Ranger Station, located a mile below the [Tahoe] Tavern." (James, *Lake*, 349.)

Zephyr: Cove, Point Nevada: Douglas
Glenbrook
South Lake Tahoe

Named for the west winds that blow over Lake Tahoe and on into Nevada. Zephyr, originating from the Greek god of the west wind, *zephuros*, is of French origin. (*OED*, vol. 2, 1357.)

Lt. M. M. Macomb cited Zephyr Cove in his report, and the name appeared on the Wheeler map of 1878. (Wheeler, *Report*, 1280.) A post office was established on July 10, 1930. (Carlson, 250.)

Mark Twain and Dan De Quille arrived in Virginia City in 1862; both wrote about the prevailing winds, called the "Washoe Zephyr."

"This was all we saw that day, for it was two o'clock, now, and according to custom the daily 'Washoe Zephyr' set in; a soaring dust drift about the size of the United States set up edgewise came with it, and the capital of Nevada Territory disappeared from view." (Twain, 127.)

"The 'zephyr' is one of the peculiar institutions of Washoe and as such is worthy of special mention. At certain seasons—generally in the fall and spring—furious gales prevail along the Comstock range. . . . A breeze of this kind will snatch a man's hat off his head and take it vertically a hundred feet into the air; then, as he stands gazing after it, the hat suddenly comes down at his feet, as though shot out of a cannon, and lies before him as a completely flattened out as though it had been struck with a sledgehammer." (De Quille, *Bonanza*, 187.)

"A Few Notes About Lake Tahoe. . . . The next point of view is Zephyr Cove, where a commodious house is built, among grand tall trees, on a level flat of ground at the head of the cove, which is the most beautiful on the lake. The shore line here is varied, grand old rocks alternate with sand beach, and nothing can be conductive of more pleasure than to go out in a boat when the lake is calm and look down into the depths of the water which covers these rocks, which seem to be so near, whilst they have depths of from fifty to sixty feet. Here you can watch the fish gambol, in all their freedom, and one can see them as plainly as if they were in a glass globe instead of at the bottom of a great lake." (*San Francisco Daily Alta California*, July 1, 1865.)

Appendix 1

Old Names

Bald Mountain see **Freel Peak**
Bawker's Peak see **Barker Peak**
Big Hill Summit see **Echo Summit**
Bigler, Lake see **Tahoe, Lake**
Bonpland, Lake see **Tahoe, Lake**
Boundary Bay see **Stateline, NV**
Camp Agassiz see **Glen Alpine**
Chambers Lodge see **McKinney**
Chinkapin see **Dollar Point**
Chinese Gardens see **China Gardens**
Coquette Island see **Fannette Island**
Cornelian Bay see **Carnelian Bay**
Crystal Peak see **Tallac, Mount**
Daggett Creek see **Haines Creek**
Daggett Pass see **Kingsbury Grade**
Desolation Valley see **Desolation Wilderness**
Devil's Basin and Valley see **Desolation Wilderness**
Dubliss Mountain see **Duane Bliss Peak**
Eagle Cliff see **Eagle Rock**
Emerald Bay Falls see **Eagle Falls**
Emerald I. see **Fannette Island**
Fleetfoot Peak see **Maggies Peaks**
Friday Creek see **Burke Creek**
Friday's Station see **Edgewood**
Gladys Lake see **Azure Lake**
Glenbrook Rocks see **Logan Shoals**
Grecian Bay see **Rubicon Bay**
Hawley's Summit see **Echo Summit**
Hobart see **Folsom**
Hot Springs Hotel see **Brockway**
Hurricane Bay see **Sunnyside**
Idlewild see **Tahoe Pines**
Island House see **Antone Meadows**
Job's Group of Mountains see **Freel Peak, Jobs Sister**
Johnson Trail Summit or Hill see **Echo Summit**
Lake House see **Al Tahoe**
Lake Stream see **Upper Truckee River**
Lake Valley Creek see **Upper Truckee River**

Appendix 2

Charles Preuss's diaries are in the Library of Congress. The following translation of a portion of one diary was made from a typed transcription that is on microfilm at the Bancroft Library, Berkeley, California. The diaries in their entirety have previously been published: Preuss, Charles. *Exploring with Frémont. The Private Diaries of Charles Preuss, Cartographer for John C. Frémont on his First, Second, and Fourth Expeditions to the Far West.* Translated and edited by Edwin G. and Elizabeth K. Gudde. Norman: University of Oklahoma Press, 1958.

Diary of Charles Preuss, January 15 to February 28, 1844

d. 15. January. During our short days' marches we reached a deep lake, but do not yet know whether it is Mary's Lake or not. The lake has no outlet, but a small river flows into it. Near where we are camping, the river is swarming with magnificent salmon-trout. We traded a few trinkets for a whole load of fish from the Indians and I almost ate myself into oblivion. The winter is rather mild here, if only the wind would not blow so often. Remarkable volcanic rocks.

d. 26. January. We are having a day of rest today, which is something of a miracle. We still don't know for sure where we are. Yesterday we crossed mountains with deep, deep snow, and for tomorrow, we are facing even higher mountains; therefore, our animals need some rest. We still don't know whether the Sacramento Valley, which we are looking for, lies behind this last range of mountains. By the way, the weather is wonderful, but very cold at night. By now I am quite used to sleeping outdoors and I don't even want to stay overnight in the smoky tent except when it rains. My oil cloth protects me sufficiently from snow and hoar frost. Nevertheless, from time to time, I feel a touch a rheumatism in my hips. We have heard that there is no real winter but only a great deal of rain in the Sacramento Valley during this season. If this is true, I have to believe that the Sacramento Valley is not behind these mountains, because the sky is incredibly blue over there.

So far there is no shortage of provisions. We are out of meat, but peas, flour, rice, sugar, and coffee keep us almost fat. We have also enough grass and water since we passed the hot springs or at least since we left the trout streams, so that my mule rivals me in being fat. My boots are in such miserable condition, that I really don't know how I can get to California in them.

d. 3. February. We are getting deeper and deeper into the mountains and snow. Now and then we give little presents to vagabond Indians to guide us across. They accompany us for a few miles and then leave us at the first opportunity. Now we have hired one who is supposed to take us all the way to the white people. Apparently we are now at the base of the mountain range which is the real divide. By tomorrow we will know whether or not we will be deceived again. The snow is so horribly deep, and we can cover only a few miles each day. I am walking almost barefoot. This surpasses all the hardships that I have experienced till now. One often had bad days with the good old Prussian Surveying Office, but one was assured of comfortable quarters in the evening. Here all we have is a buffalo hide on the snow as our bed.

d. 6. February. We have already spent two days at the top of the range. The snow prevents us from continuing. The horses are further down trying to scratch up a little grass. One group led by our Great Leader [Feldherrn] started out on snowshoes today to break a trail to the summit, which seems to be 10 miles away. Tomorrow we will probably learn whether we can get through here. Yesterday our people had a terrible job dragging our packs up a steep mountain, because our animals are too weak. Two of them rolled down the snow 100 feet just as we children did without hurting ourselves during the summer at the Krummer House near Detmold.

No more salt in the camp. Disgusting.

d. 8. February. Sacramento Valley is discovered. Slowly we work through the snow. Sleds and snowshoes make a good enough track that probably the unladen horses will be able to get across. Our people are now the pack horses. It was impossible to sleep last night, all the blankets and all the hides could not keep one warm. In the daytime it is wonderful.

The local Indians live almost exclusively on firseeds [Pinyon pine, *Pinus monophylla*], which are tasty and oily. For special treats they eat mice and rats.—Robbed by our guide; left bow and arrows behind.— Left the cannon behind a few days ago.

d. 11. February. We are now all snowed in. The snowstorm is upon us. The strong wind is burying the tracks which we had made with immense effort for our horses. The horses are about 20 miles from us and we expect them to arrive this evening, or, rather we no longer expect them anymore. —How could they get through? No one can say at this moment how things are going to turn out. One thing is sure, we will have to eat horsemeat. I don't care if we have horsemeat; all I want is salt. I feel pretty weak and have little appetite.

d. 13. February. This situation has a definite, but unpleasant outlook.

The day before yesterday an attempt was made to take the horses through. A few were led forward, the others followed calmly, but not for long. The lead horse broke through the packed snow. In his attempt to get out of it, he sank even deeper, the same happened to some of the horses in the middle of the train. This frightened the others and they left the track and sank up to their ears in the snow. In short it soon became such a mess that we had to make much more careful attempts to bring the horses back into the track. We got this news from Fitz, who was in camp 8 miles back, where the deep snow begins. We, the lower six men, are camped 3 miles from the summit.

When F[rémont] received the bad news, the following plan was made. Immediately we had to start packing down the snow as much as we could with our feet and mauls. We threw heavy branches on the track. In the meantime, five men were sent back with the horses to an area where grass and water are available (12 miles to the east from Fitz's camp). A few of the horses were slaughtered immediately so that our people can maintain their strength, and we could use the meager amount of flour and peas sparingly. The former no longer in the shape of bread, but as horsemeat soup.

Fitz had already slaughtered one skinny horse, and along with some meat, he had sent us the bad news. I ate some of it yesterday. I can't say if it tasted good or not. There was no fat on the meat, (it is supposed to taste pretty bad). As far as I am concerned unsalted food never tastes good to me. The second victim was my poor Jack being the fattest mule. Last night we received a sled full of this meat, and I haven't eaten any of it, nor do I want to. We had to wait so long for the meat, that Alex was afraid he would have to go to work without his meat breakfast; therefore, he grabbed little Clammet [a dog from the Klamath area] by the fur and killed him. The dog was prepared in the Indian fashion, the hair was singed off and [it was] scalded (awful stench in our kitchen), cleaned the skin with water and soap and then with snow (Alex paraded around the meat happily looking at the golden-yellow skin, Heavens [*ach*]!)

When we arrived here we set fire to an old thick fir [pine], which soon melted the snow around it. These two snowless holes are now our living area and kitchen. (I prefer the open kitchen to the smoky cubbyhole.) The present situation is as follows: F[rémont] went with 4 others to work on the trail. I lie in the kitchen hole on my buffalo hide near the fire to watch that the food does not get burned. Two pots and a tea kettle are in front of the fire. In one of the pots are the peas and the chopped up meat of my Jack, and in the other, a smaller pot, half of the dog. The tea kettle is full of snow water with which I keep the pots simmering, a process which Alex has especially recommended. When the others return everything will be tender. Then bread will be baked with sugar instead of salt, at least we still have that in our flour. We will make some good coffee and have our meal.

If I should also tell you about my inner man, then I must tell you that my stomach is in bad condition. I think the lack of salt is to blame for it and I am so dammed weak. Yesterday I went the 3 miles to the peak to look down into the promised land, and it took me a dreadfully long time to work my way through the snow. I had to rest several times and returned utterly exhausted. I totally lack appetite and therefore, I cannot eat the meat, and hardly can manage the saltless peas, and that little bit of bread gives no strength. How long it will take to get through here, and whether we will be able to bring our horses through on this new icy track, only time can tell.

In the valley on the other side everything was dense fog yesterday and one could only faintly make out another lower mountain range which, according to Kid [Kit], lies between the Sacramento Valley and the ocean. Our astronomical observations confirm this. Although I doubt the accuracy of the longitude, our latitude, as well as the one indicated on the map for San Francisco Bay, must be correct. My estimate of the distance from the highest point to the foot of the mountain range is 30 miles. We shall see, and also whether we can descend the other side of the ridge, where the wind has blown away the snow.

This is all for the moment. I'll give the dog a little water, and then pick up Byron's Don Juan.

d. 15. February. Same situation. Just received the news that 51 of our remaining 63 animals have succeeded in getting across the 4 miles we had built. Since it thawed last night, it turned out to be a difficult project! The track had to be packed down again. The little dog tasted good, but the great happy news is that our people obtained rock salt by trading with the Indians. Just now Taplin brought a big chunk of it.

d. 16. February. My poor jack has been consumed, I did not eat any of it. Today a horse will be killed, and now that we have some salt, I am looking forward to eating. This is the end of baking bread, there are only a few handfuls of flour left to thicken the horsemeat pea soup. F[rémont] has such an appetite that even between meals a skewer with meat is kept by the fire for him. Today he went with Jacob to reconnoiter the area to the west. Our people make tracks for the horses, because there is very little grass where they are. I am told that the horses look like real skeletons. I haven't seen them for 3 weeks.

d. 18. February. Still in the old snow hole. The horses are now near us on a snow-free hill, where there is supposed to be adequate grass. The sun does its work in melting the snow day by day. F[rémont] did not make any big discoveries, yet it seems that we will be able to traverse several mountain ranges as soon as we are over the divide. We are constantly packing down the track. The horsemeat is satisfactory as long as our supply of salt holds out. My appetite has returned. I wish I had something to still it.

Our latitude is 38° 41'.

Good appetite, always in the free mountain air, only two meals, nothing but peas and horsemeat—what a strange combination. I wish I were in the market with a basket, how I would relish the shopping.

d. 21. February. Today we have crossed the ridges with our miserable animals. (From the original 104 only 53 survived, of which another 3 to 4 will most likely be slaughtered.) We are looking into the distant valley, from where relief must come. Seemingly, we will not have any more problems with the snow. (Down in the valley there is a thunderstorm and it is raining.) Even here the weather is milder.

However, the lower mountains through which and over which we have to wend our way look damn rocky. Were it not for the pathetic animals, without which we could not have our baggage, we probably could reach the valley in two days. Things being what they are—God knows how long it will take.

d. 22. February. Today once again we had to work our way through the snow, alternating with rocky terrain. Two animals got stuck. We covered another 3 miles. But what weather. Such sunrises and beautiful dawns and dusks, one never sees in the area around Hanover. I notice in Gustav's little pocket atlas that we are at the same latitude as Palermo [Sicily] and Smyrna [Turkey]. The sky like forget-me-nots.

When a horse has to be shot, as just happened, it tears me apart. Every day and a half one is devoured. Our people have nothing else, and you can imagine that it does not make a juicy roast. If only our supply of peas would last until we reach the valley. I would be content. How lovely it sounds when a fat buffalo cow must give up her life, quite a different sound. Louis repaired a pair of moccasins with a piece of leather from his saddle. Now things are going better and I can climb the rocks easily. What luck, we still have tobacco, as bad as it is.

d. 24. February. We are out of the snow at last, yesterday was still a bad day. Snow, rocks, underbrush. Terrible marching. In 9 hours we made 3 miles, until we came to where another branch flows into the river. From there we descended the steep slope facing to the south, (which means the ridge goes from west to east), and the sun has melted almost all of the snow. Up and down it was very steep, especially where we had to cross gorges, but overall, forest ground and firs etc., and in between enormous boulders are strewn. We made about 12 miles in four hours and we find here some grass and horsetail reeds for our hungry animals. We stopped here, because such places are rare in these woods. Another horse was shot just now, hopefully we will soon come to the end of this eating of horses. Tomorrow I think we should be quite near the valley, and my Polly can recover feeding on good grass so that I can ride her again. Walking is getting somewhat difficult. Horsemeat does not give you strength, and as every naturalist knows peas have little nutritional value. (P.S. One mule was so hungry that he ate the tail of Fitz's horse plus part of the saddle and my reins, etc.)

d. 25. February. Eight of us plus the best of our miserable animals separated ourselves from the rest of the group in order to make faster progress. There is not enough grass to feed them all at one spot. We made about 12 miles and stopped at a little place where there is good grass (green from last year, preserved by the snow). Instead of snow we have a strong rain shower (which is not pleasant either). I was glad to find an old Indian hut where I made my bed. I'm afraid that the rain will again drive me into the damn cubbyhole for some time. Splendid trees grow here. We measured the circumference of the cedar (Juniper) at 28½ feet 4 feet from the ground. In my system of botany I called this tree a pencil tree, because pencils are made of its wood. Live oaks are common around here, not a beautiful tree, but a very useful tree, especially as lumber for building ships. The leaves are quite different, not in the least similar to the other oaks.

d. 28. February. In the morning. The day before yesterday we still had a bad trip across rocks, etc. and stopped by a torrential arm of the river, which we crossed yesterday in the morning after trying at various places to get across. The horses were bedded down without eating grass. They were so weak yesterday that we had to carry the packs up hill and put them back on the animals at the top; fortunately, 2 miles from yesterday's camp we found some green grass which will strengthen them. Day before yesterday I found the first flowers. . . ."

Illustration Sources

5	CHS	FN-14510
7	NHS	Ethnic #505
15	CHS	FN-26712
18	CHS	FN-28852
20	CHS	FN-09543
22	CHS	FN-28864
		(USGS Bulletin 612, Plate XLVI.)
26	CSL	NEG #8516
29	BL	8516
33	BL	1905.16420 STER
41	Hildinger, Jim	
43	BL	11598 PIC
45	CHS	FN-28877
46	NHS	Portrait
54	Hildinger, Jim	
56	CSL	#9671
63	CHS	FN-02479
64	NHS	Industry-Lumbering #44
75	NHS	Biog. P-173
79	CHS	FN-26827 c1
82	CHS	FN-26711
83	Hildinger, Jim	100-73
85	CSL	NEG #9269
100	CHS	FN-28851 c1
106	CHS	FN-26388
109	NHS	Lake Tahoe NEG #468
113	BL	Portrait
117	BL	12 1845e F
119	BL	12 1848 B copy 2
120	BL	Map 4 P7 1850c B
121	BL	15 C2 1857 B
122	BL	15.N3(w) 1860b B
125	BL	15 N3 1863 C
128	BL	Map 12 1863a D
131	BL	2214 PIC
131	CHS	FN-28854
134	CSL	NEG #9672
138	NHS	BIOG T-42
146	Hildinger, Jim	91-71
150	CHS	FN-28856
		(USGS Bulletin 612, Plate XLV.)

Bibliography

Angel, *Nevada*. Angel, Myron, ed. *History of Nevada*, 1881. Reprint. Berkeley: Howell-North Books, 1958.

Angel, *Placer*. Angel, Myron. *History of Placer County California*. Oakland: Thompson & West, 1882.

Ayers. Ayers, R. W. *Origin of Name and Date of Creation of the National Forests of the California Region*. US Forest Service, Division of Information and Education, 1940.

Bailey. Bailey, G. E. "The History, Origin and Meaning of Some California Towns and Places," *Overland Monthly* 44, nos. 4 & 5, October & November 1904: 469–478, 558–567.

Bancroft. Bancroft, H. H. *History of California*. vol. III. 1825–1840. San Francisco: The History Company, 1886.

Bancroft's Map, 1863. *Bancroft's Map of the Pacific States*. Compiled by Wm. H. Knight, 1863. Bancroft Library.

Bartlett's Map, 1854. *General Map Showing the Countries Explored & Surveyed by the United States & Mexican Boundary Commission, in the years 1850, 51, 52, & 53, Under the direction of John R. Bartlett, U.S. Commissioner*, 1854. Bancroft Library.

BGN. United States Board on Geographic Names. *Decisions* 8503, 1985. Washington: Department of the Interior, 1985.

BGN, *Sixth Report*. *Sixth Report of the United States Geographic Board, 1890 to 1932*. Washington: Government Printing Office, 1933.

Bixler. Bixler, W. K. *A Dozen Sierra Success Stories*. Tahoe Valley: Sierra Publishing, 1964.

Bloss. Bloss, Roy S. *Pony Express-The Great Gamble*. Berkeley: Howell-North, 1959.

Bradley. Bradley, Cornelius B. "Knapsack Tours in the Sierra," *Sierra Club Bulletin* 1, no. 8, May 1896: 315–24.

Brewer, *Field Notes.* Brewer, William H. *Field Notes, Geology.* Manuscript C-B 1069, Bancroft Library.

Brewer, *Observations.* Brewer, William H. *Field Notes and Observations.* Manuscript C-B 320, Bancroft Library.

Brewer, *Up and Down.* Brewer, William H. *Up and Down California in 1860–1864: the Journal of William H. Brewer.* Edited by Francis P. Farquhar. 3d ed. Berkeley and Los Angeles: University of California Press, 1966.

Britannica. *Encyclopaedia Britannica.* Chicago: William Benton Publisher, 1966.

Browning. Browning, Peter. *Place Names of the Sierra Nevada.* Berkeley: Wilderness Press, 1986.

California. *California Historical Landmarks.* Department of Parks and Recreation. Sacramento: California Office of State Printing, 1968.

California Blue Book. Curry, Charles Forrest. *California Blue Book or State Roster.* Sacramento: State Printing Office, 1909.

Carlson. Carlson, Helen S. *Nevada Place Names.* Reno: University of Nevada Press, 1974.

Carson. Carson, Christopher. *Kit Carson's Autobiography.* Edited with an introduction by Milo Milton Quaife. Lincoln: University of Nebraska Press, 1966.

Carter. Carter, Kate B. *Utah and the Pony Express.* Salt Lake City: Utah Pony Express Centennial Commission, 1960.

Challinor. Challinor, John. *A Dictionary of Geology.* Fifth Edition. Cardiff: University of Wales Press. New York: Oxford University Press, 1978.

Clarke. Clarke, Clinton C. *Pacific Crest Trailway.* Pasadena: Pacific Crest Trail System Conference, 1945.

Coy. Coy, Owen C. *California County Boundaries.* rev. ed. Berkeley: California Historical Survey Commission, 1973.

Craven. Craven, Bill. "Profile Bill Craven: Keeper of Fallen Leaf History," *Keep Tahoe Blue,* January 1988: 11–12.

Crocker. Charles Crocker letter to John W. Dwinelle, October 17, 1879. Manuscript C-Y 51, Bancroft Library.

Crosley. Crosley, Mary Edith. *Coloma.* Universal City, California: Crosley Books, 1958.

CSL. California State Library, California Room, Sacramento.

Davidson. Davidson, George. "The Origin and the Meaning of the Name California." *Transactions and Proceedings of the Geographical Society of the Pacific* 6, part 1, series 2, 1910.

Davis, *Nevada*. Davis, Sam P., ed. *The History of Nevada*. 2 vols. Reno and Los Angeles: The Elms Publishing Co., Inc., 1913.

Davis, *Sacramento*. Davis, Hon. Win. J. *An Illustrated History of Sacramento County, California*. Chicago: The Lewis Publishing Co., 1890.

d'Azevedo. d'Azevedo, Warren L. "The Washo Indians of California and Nevada," *University of Utah Anthropological Papers* 67, Aug. 1963: 1–201.

De Groot's Map, 1860. *De Groot's Map of the Washoe Mines*, 1860. (3d Edition, 1862.) Bancroft Library.

De Groot's Map, 1863. *A Tracing of a Map of Nevada & Eastern California*. Compiled by Dr. De Groot, 1863.

DeLaguna. DeLaguna, F. "The California Lake Country," *Out West* 19, no. 3, September 1903: 262–68.

De Quille, *Bonanza*. De Quille, Dan (William Wright). *The Big Bonanza*. New York: Alfred A. Knopf, 1947.

De Quille, *Comstock*. De Quille, Dan (William Wright). *A History of the Comstock Silver Lode and Mines*. New York: Promontory Press, 1974.

DFG. California Department of Fish and Game, Lake Reports, Rancho Cordova.

Downs. Downs, James F. *Two Worlds of the Washo*. New York: Holt, Rinehart and Winston, 1966.

Eden. Letter from Velma Comstock Eden to the author, 1988.

Edwards. Edwards, W. F. *Edwards' Tourists' Guide and Directory of the Truckee Basin*. Truckee: Republican Job Print, 1883.

Farquhar, *Frémont*. Farquhar, Francis P. "Frémont in the Sierra Nevada," *Sierra Club Bulletin* 15, no. 1, February 1930: 74–95.

Farquhar, *Sierra*. Farquhar, Francis P. *History of the Sierra Nevada*. Berkeley and Los Angeles: University of California Press, 1965.

Fisher. Fisher, Walter K. "William Wightman Price," *The Condor* 25, March 1923: 50–57.

Font's Map of 1776. *Mapa correspondiente al diario que formo el P.F. Pedro Font del viage que hizo a Monterey y puerto de San Francisco. P.F. Petrus Font fecit Ures anno 1776*. Bancroft Library.

Freed, *Aboriginal*. Freed, Stanley A. and Ruth S. Freed. "A Configuration of Aboriginal Washo Culture," in "The Washo Indians of California and Nevada." *University of Utah Anthropological Papers* 67, Aug. 1963: 41–56.

Freed, *Washo*. Freed, Stanley A. "Washo Habitation Sites In the Lake Tahoe Area," *Reports of the University of California Archaeological Survey. Notes on Western Nevada Archaeology and Ethnology* 66, February 1966: 73–83.

Frémont, *Expedition*. Frémont, John Charles. *Report of the Exploring Expedition to the Rocky Mountains in the year 1842, and to Oregon and North California in the years 1843–44*. Washington, 1845. (U.S. 28th Cong., 2d sess. House Ex. doc. no. 166.)

Frémont, *Geographical*. Frémont, John Charles. *Geographical Memoir Upon Upper California*. Washington, 1848. (U.S. 30th Cong. 1st sess. Senate Misc. doc. no. 148.) Reprint Edition with Introductions by Allan Nevins and Dale L. Morgan and a Reproduction of the Map. San Francisco: The Book Club of California, 1964.

Frémont Map, 1845. *Map of an Exploring Expedition to the Rocky Mountains in the Year 1842 and to Oregon & North California in the Years 1843–44.*

Frémont Map, 1848. *Map of Oregon and Upper California From the Surveys of John Charles Frémont And other Authorities drawn by Charles Preuss Under the Order of the Senate of the United States Washington City 1848.*

Frémont, *Memoirs*. Frémont, John Charles. *Memoirs of My Life*. Chicago and New York: Belford, Clarke & Co., 1887.

Gibbes' Map. Gibbes, Charles Drayton. *Map of Alpine Co. and Mining Districts*, 1866. Bancroft Library.

Goddard, *Bigler*. Goddard, George H. "Bigler Lake," *Hutchings' California Magazine* 2, no. 3, September 1857: 107–9.

Goddard, *Report*. Goddard, George H. *Report of a Survey of a portion of the Eastern boundary of California, and a Reconnaissance of the old Carson and Johnson immigrant roads over the Sierra Nevada*. To the Honorable S. H. Marlette, Survey-General. Sacramento: State Printing Office, Dec. 15, 1855.

Goddard, *Sierra*. Goddard, George H. *Portion of Sierra Nevada range, California and Nevada*. Copy from G. H. Goddard's maps of 1855 and 1853.

Goddard, *South*. Goddard, George H. *Sierra region south of Lake Tahoe. From G. H. Goddard's Triangulation* [of 1855?]. Published circa 1870.

Goodwin. Goodwin, Charles Carroll. *As I Remember Them*. Salt Lake City: Special Committee of the Salt Lake Commerce Club, 1913.

Great Register. *Great Register El Dorado County, 1872/1873*. Bancroft Library.

Greuner. Greuner, Lorene. *Lake Valley's Past*. South Lake Tahoe, California: Lake Tahoe Historical Society, 1976.

Gudde. Gudde, Erwin G. *California Place Names*. 3d ed., rev. Berkeley and Los Angeles: University of California Press, 1969.

Guinn. Guinn, James Miller. *A History of California and an Extended History of its Southern Coast Counties*. 2 vols. Los Angeles: Historic Record Co., 1907.

Hanna. Hanna, Phil Townsend. *Dictionary of California Land Names*. Los Angeles: Automobile Club of Southern California, 1946.

Hart. Hart, James D. *A Companion to California*. New York: Oxford University Press, 1978.

Hawley. Hawley, A. H. *Lake Tahoe*. San Francisco, California, 1883. Manuscript P-G 4, Bancroft Library.

Hazard. Hazard, Joseph T. *Pacific Crest Trails from Alaska to Cape Horn*. Seattle: Superior Publishing Company, 1946.

Henderson. Henderson, William. "Report of Committee on Internal Improvements," Exhibit A. February 23, 1855. *Pamphlets on California* 8, no. 5: 8–10. Bancroft Library. (F858 C21, v. 8 x.)

Hildebrand. Hildebrand, Joel Henry. "A History of Skiing in California," *The British Ski Year Book* 10, no. 20, 1939: 64–78.

Hildinger. Letter from Jim Hildinger to the author, 1987.

Hittell, *History*. Hittell, John S. *History of California*. San Francisco: H. H. Bancroft Co., 1887.

Hittell, *Pacific*. Hittell, John S. *Handbook of Pacific Coast Travel*. San Francisco: H. H. Bancroft & Co., 1887.

Hoffmann's 1873 Map. *Topographical map of Central California, together with a part of Nevada*, 1873. Charles F. Hoffmann, Principal Topographer. State Geological Survey of California. Bancroft Library.

Hoover. Hoover, Mildred Brooke; Rensch, Hero Eugene; and Rensch, Ethel Grace. *Historic Spots in California*. 3d ed. Revised by William N. Abeloe. Stanford: Stanford University Press, 1966.

Hopkins. Hopkins, Sarah Winnemucca. *Life Among the Paiutes*. New York: G.P. Putnam's Sons, 1883.

Hutchinson. Hutchinson, Lincoln. "A Tramp in the Emerald Bay Region," *Sierra Club Bulletin* 2, no. 1, January 1897: 56–57.

Ives, Houghton & Kidder Map. Butler Ives, J. F. Houghton, and John F. Kidder. *Map of the Boundary Line between California and Nevada Territory*, as surveyed, 1863. Bancroft Library.

Jackson. Jackson, Helen Hunt. *Bits of Travel at Home*. Boston: Robert Bros., 1878.

James, *Heroes*. James, George Wharton. *Heroes of California*. Boston: Little, Brown, & Co., 1910.

James, *Lake*. James, George Wharton. *Lake Tahoe: Lake of the Sky*. Chicago: Charles T. Powner Co., 1956.

Kent. Kent, Elizabeth Thacker. *William Kent, Independent, a Biography*. Kentfield, California: 1950.

King. King, Thomas Starr. *Christianity and Humanity*. Edited by Edwin P. Whipple. Boston: Houghton, Mifflin, 1897.

Knight. Knight, William Henry. "An Emigrant's Trip Across the Plains," *Historical Society of Southern California* 12, no. 3, 1923: 32–41.

Kroeber, *Indians*. Kroeber, Alfred Louis. *Handbook of the Indians of California*, Reprint edition. Berkeley: California Book Company, Ltd., 1953.

Kroeber, *Names*. Kroeber, Alfred Louis, "California Place Names of Indian Origin," *University of California Publications in American Archaeology and Ethnology* 12, no. 2, June 15, 1916: 31–69.

Kroeber, *Shoshonean*. Kroeber, Alfred Louis. "The Shoshonean Dialects of California," *University of California Publications in American Archaeology and Ethnology* 4, no. 3, February 1907: 65–166.

Kroeber, *Washo*. Kroeber, Alfred Louis. "The Washo Language of East Central California and Nevada," *University of California Publications in American Archaeology and Ethnology* 4, no. 5, September 1907: 251–318.

Lamar. Lamar, Howard R. *The Reader's Encyclopedia of the American West*. New York: Thomas Y. Crowell Co., 1977.

Landmarks. *California Historical Landmarks*. Department of Parks and Recreation. Sacramento: California Office of State Printing, 1968.

Lawson and Ives Township Lines Nevada, September 1861. Nevada Historical Society, Reno.

LeConte, *Studies*. LeConte, John. "Physical Studies of Lake Tahoe, Parts I-III," *Overland Monthly* 2 & 3, November 1883, December 1883, and January 1884: 506–17; 595–612; 41–46.

LeConte, *Glaciers*. LeConte, Joseph. "On Some of the Ancient Glaciers of the Sierra Nevada," Third Series, *American Journal of Science and Arts* 10, 1875: 126–39.

LeConte, *Ramblings*. LeConte, Joseph. "Ramblings through the High Sierra," *Sierra Club Bulletin* 3, no. 1, Jan. 1900: 1–107. (LeConte's journal was privately printed in 1875, and later republished as *A Journal of Ramblings Through the High Sierra of California*. San Francisco: Sierra Club, 1960.)

MacDonald. MacDonald, Claire. *Lake Tahoe, California*. Mount Vernon, New York: Privately printed, 1929.

Map of the Carson Valley. USGS, *Map of the Carson Valley*, Comstock Mining and Miners, Plate II, 1883. Bancroft Library.

Map of the Comstock Area, ca. 1875. Bancroft Library.

Macomb. Lieutenant Montgomery Meigs Macomb (1852–1924), Fourth Artillery, US Army, in charge of the Wheeler Survey field party in California, 1876, 1877, and 1878. See **Wheeler, *Report.***

Markham. Markham, Edwin. *California the Wonderful*. New York: Hearst's Intl. Co., 1914.

Marlette. Marlette, S. H. *Annual Report of the Surveyor General of California for 1855*. See **Goddard, *Report***.

Maule. Maule, William M. *A Contribution to the Geographic and Economic History of the Carson, Walker and Mono Basins in Nevada and California*. San Francisco: US Forest Service, 1938.

Merriam. Merriam, C. Hart. "First Crossing of the Sierra Nevada: Jedediah Smith's Trip From California to Salt Lake in 1827," *Sierra Club Bulletin* 11, no. 4, 1923: 375–79.

Mighels. Mighels, Henry R. *Sage Brush Leaves*. San Francisco: Edward Bosqui & Co. Printers, 1879.

Miller. Miller, Loye Holmes, letters. Manuscript 67/209/c, Bancroft Library.

Myrick. Myrick, David F. *Railroads of Nevada and Eastern California. Volume One-The Northern Roads.* Berkeley: Howell-North Books, 1962.

Nevers. Nevers, Jo Ann. *Wa She Shu: A Washo Tribal History*. Reno: Inter-Tribal Council of Nevada, 1976.

OED. *The Compact Edition of the Oxford English Dictionary*. 2 vols. New York: Oxford University Press, 1971.

Oxford. Milford, H. S. *The Oxford Book of English Verse of the Romantic Period*. London: Oxford University Press, 1928.

Partridge. Partridge, Eric. *Origins*. 2d ed. New York: Macmillan Co., 1958.

Preuss maps. For Preuss maps, see Frémont.

Preuss. The diary of Charles Preuss, translated by Monica Clyde, Hans Hollitscher, and Helmi Nock. See Appendix 2.

Price, *Washo*. Price, John A. "Washo Prehistory, A Review of Research," *University of Utah Anthropological Papers* no. 67, Aug. 1963: 77–95.

Price, *Glen Alpine*. Price, W. W. *Glen Alpine Lake Tahoe Forest Reserve California*. San Francisco: Pillsbury Picture Co., 1906.

Price, *Guide*. Price, W. W. *A Guide to the Lake Tahoe Region*. San Francisco: A. S. Pillsbury, 1902.

Putnam. Putnam, Ruth, with the collaboration of Herbert I. Priestly. "California: The Name," *University of California Publications in History* 4, no. 4, December 19, 1917: 293–365.

Reed's map. Reed, Theron. *Map of the Silver Mountain Mining District*, 1864. Bancroft Library.

Reimer. Reimer, George. *Col. A. W. Von Schmidt; His Career as Surveyor and Engineer, 1852–1900.* M.A. Thesis in History, June 1961. Bancroft Library.

Rider. Rider, Fremont. *Rider's California; A Guide-book for Travelers*. New York: The Macmillan Co., 1925.

Salley. Salley, H. E. *History of California Post Offices, 1849–1976*. La Mesa, CA: Heartland Printing and Publishing Co., 1977.

Sanchez. Sanchez, Nellie Van de Grift. *Spanish and Indian Place Names of California*. San Francisco: A. M. Robertson, 1914.

Schrepfer. Schrepfer, Susan R. *The Fight To Save the Redwoods*. Madison: University of Wisconsin Press, 1983.

Schuster. Schuster, Addison Brown. "The Knave: El Dorado Names," *Oakland Tribune*, July 23, 1944.

Schwenke. Schwenke, Karl and Thomas Winnett. *Sierra North*. 2d ed., Berkeley: Wilderness Press, 1971.

Scott. Scott, Edward B. *The Saga of Lake Tahoe*. Eighth ed. Crystal Bay, Nevada: Sierra-Tahoe Publishing Co., 1964.

Shinn. Shinn, Charles Howard. *The Story of the Mine as Illustrated by the Great Comstock Lode of Nevada*. New York: Appleton & Co., 1896.

Shumate. Shumate, Albert. *The Life of George Henry Goddard*. Berkeley: Friends of the Bancroft Library University of California, 1969.

Sierra Highlands. *Sierra Highlands*. San Francisco: H. S. Crocker Co., n. d.

Simpson, *California*. Simpson, J. H. *The Shortest Route to California Illustrated by a History of Explorations of the Great Basin of Utah with its Topographical and Geological Character and Some Account of the Indian Tribes*. Philadelphia: J. B. Lippincott & Co., 1869.

Simpson, *Route*. Simpson, J. H. *Report of Explorations Across the Great Basin of the Territory of Utah for a Direct Wagon-Route from Camp Floyd to Genoa, in Carson Valley in 1859*. Washington: Government Printing Office, 1876.

Sioli. Sioli, Paolo. *Historical Souvenir of El Dorado County, California, with Illustrations and Biographical Sketches of its Prominent Men and Pioneers*. Oakland: Paolo Sioli, 1883.

Statutes. *Statutes of California*. Statutes of 1869–70, Chapter 58, 64. Statutes of 1945, Chapter 1499, 2777.

Stewart, *Names*. Stewart, George R. *Names on the Land*. 4th ed. San Francisco: Lexikos, 1982.

Stewart, *Trail*. Stewart, George R. *The California Trail*. New York: McGraw-Hill Book Co., 1962.

Storer. Storer, Tracy I. and Robert L. Usinger. *Sierra Nevada Natural History, An Illustrated Handbook*. Berkeley and Los Angeles: University of California Press, 1963.

Strong. Strong, Douglas Hillman. *Tahoe, An Environmental History*. Lincoln: University of Nebraska Press, 1984.

Swanton. Swanton, John R. "The Indian Tribes of North America," *Smithsonian Institution Bureau of American Ethnology Bulletin* 145. Washington: USGPO, 1952.

Talbot. Letter from Georg J. Talbot to Irene Bhuitt, July 8, 1907. Bancroft Library.

Taylor. Taylor, Bayard. *El Dorado, or, Adventures in the Path of Empire: Comprising a Voyage to California, via Panama; Life in San Francisco and Monterey; Pictures of the Gold Region, and Experiences of Mexican Travel*. 2 vols. New York: George P. Putnam, 1850.

Teather. Teather, Louise. *Discovering Marin*. Fairfax, California: Tamal Land Press, 1974.

Teggart. Teggart, Frederick J., ed. "The Anza Expedition of 1775–1776, Diary of Pedro Font," *Publications of the Academy of Pacific Coast History* 3, no. 1, March 1913. Berkeley: University of California, March 1913.

Turner. Turner, Henry W. "Further Contributions to the Geology of the Sierra Nevada," *Seventeenth Annual Report of the USGS*, 1895–1896, Part I. Washington: GPO, 1896.

Twain. Twain, Mark. *Roughing It*. New York: Harper & Bros., 1913.

Upton. Upton, Charles Elmer. *Pioneers of El Dorado*. Placerville, California: Charles Elmer Upton Publisher, 1906.

USFS. US Forest Service. Lake Tahoe Basin Management Unit, South Lake Tahoe.

USGS. US Geological Survey. Quad Reports. Menlo Park, California.

USGS Bulletin. Lee, Willis T., et al. USGS Bulletin 612. *Guidebook of the Western United States. Part B. The Overland Route, with a side trip to Yellowstone Park*. Washington: Government Printing Office, 1916.

Uzes. Uzes, Francois D. *Chaining the Land, A History of Surveying in California*. Sacramento: Landmark Enterprises, 1977.